THE PICK OF PATRICK'S PANTRY

Recipes by Patrick Anthony

ANGLIA TELEVISION

INTRODUCTION

Welcome to the Pick of Patrick's Pantry

This is the largest collection to date with 134 recipes, all of which have passed the 'screen test' on Anglia News. As regular viewers will know each edition is recorded on location somewhere in the Anglia region. 'Borrowed' kitchens have ranged from the Royal Estate at Sandringham and almost every National Trust stately home to a faithfully restored fen worker's cottage at Wicken Fen and the equally evocative Fisherman's Museum at Cromer.

Special thanks are due to the great number of kind-hearted people who have generously allowed me and my cameraman into their kitchens in order to present each week's recipes. It is a much appreciated privilege and a great pleasure to be welcomed into the heart of so many homes.

As for the food, I'm sure we've all noticed how in the past decade it has become faster, lighter, more colourful and totally international; in fact, food has never before been so frequently debated and celebrated. The astonishingly wide range of choice and availability has resulted in no scarcity either of 'star' chefs eager to show what they can do.

My own approach remains as always to demonstrate what you can do and hopefully this collection will provide for you and yours many happy hours in the kitchen and around the dining table.

PATRICK ANTHONY

CONTENTS

MEAT

PORK FILLET FANTASY

Method

Heat the oil in a large flameproof casserole, add the pork, onion, oregano and five spice powder. Cook over a moderate heat until the meat is lightly browned and the onions softened.

Cube the aubergine and add to the casserole with the courgettes, tomatoes, stock, tomato puree, soy sauce if used, crushed garlic and seasoning.

Bring to the boil, cover and bake in the oven at 350°F/180°C/gas mark 4 for 35 minutes until the meat and vegetables are tender.

If necessary and liked, the liquid can be thickened with cornflour in the usual way.

Serve garnished with finely chopped parsley accompanied with either boiled rice, potatoes or crusty bread.

Ingredients

2 tbsp oil
1lb (450g) lean pork fillet, sliced
1 onion, chopped
1 level tsp dried oregano
1 heaped tsp five spice powder
1 medium aubergine
10 oz (275g) courgettes, sliced or diced large
14 oz (400g) can chopped tomatoes
12 fl oz (330ml) chicken stock
1 level tbsp tomato puree
1 tbsp soy sauce (optional)
1 clove garlic, crushed
salt and pepper

NEW BLANQUETTE OF LAMB

Ingredients

1 tbsp oil
1 oz (25g) butter
1¼-1½ lb (600-700g) lamb, cubed, trimmed of fat (see note)
salt and pepper
8 oz (225g) onions, (small pickling onions or shallots would be good, peeled and halved or quartered)
8 oz (225g) carrots, cut into half inch chunks
2-3 cloves garlic, crushed or chopped
1 tsp or 2 sprigs thyme
2 bay leaves
1 heaped tbsp flour
½ pint (300ml) dry white wine
¾ pint (450ml) chicken stock
6 oz (175g) mushrooms (whole)
2 tbsp lemon juice
1 egg yolk
4 tbsp double cream
chopped parsley

Method

In a large flameproof casserole or pot, gently heat the oil and butter, then add the lamb pieces in 3-4 batches, simply allowing them to change colour on all sides without scorching.

Transfer each batch to a waiting dish and season with salt and pepper. If necessary, add another ½ oz (15g) of butter to the casserole and introduce the onions. Stir-fry *gently* for 1 minute, then add the carrots. Stir together and, on a moderate heat, cook for about 5 minutes.

Then add the garlic, thyme and bay leaves, stir for another minute or so and then add the meat. Mix through and increase the heat to medium hot.

Stir in the flour and add the wine. Allow to boil and then simmer for 5 minutes before adding the hot stock. Mix through, bring to the boil then reduce to a simmer, cover and cook until the meat is completely tender.

Meanwhile in another saucepan gently poach the mushrooms for 5 minutes in 2 tablespoons of water, a little salt and 1 tablespoon of lemon juice. These are to be added when the meat is tender.

As soon as the lamb is cooked, in a bowl mix together the remaining lemon juice, egg yolk and cream. Turn off the heat, add the mushrooms and then quickly stir through the cream mixture, after which a gentle re-heating may be allowed if wished.

Serve with boiled rice, a green vegetable and a good sprinkling of chopped parsley.

• In the programme I used leg of lamb, but shoulder could be equally successful or lean cubed pork.

SPARE RIB SENSATION

Method

Heat the oil in a pan and fry the onion and garlic until soft, but not browned. Remove from the pan and transfer to a flameproof casserole dish.

Coat the chops and kidney in seasoned flour and fry until browned. Add to the casserole along with the salami. Add the beans, stock, tomato puree and paprika and stir through well.

Bring to the boil, stir in the thyme and seasoning and then simmer gently for 1¾ hours, or until the chops are tender. Sprinkle with chopped parsley before serving.

Accompany with baked potatoes and a green vegetable.

Ingredients

2 tbsp oil
1 onion, finely chopped
2 cloves garlic, crushed
4 spare rib chops
1 pork kidney, cut into large pieces
2 tbsp seasoned flour
2 oz (50g) salami slices
2 x 14 oz (400g) cans butter beans, drained
¾ pint (450ml) pork stock **or** chicken stock
3 tbsp tomato puree
1 level tbsp paprika
1 tsp dried thyme
salt and pepper
chopped parsley

PORK FILLET
with Bombay Cream

Method

Heat the oil in a large frying pan and add the pork fillets allowing to brown well on all sides.

Transfer pork to an ovenproof dish, sprinkle with salt and pepper and ground coriander if using, and cook in the oven at 375°F/190°C/gas mark 5 for 30 minutes.

Pour off any excess fat from the frying pan and return to the heat. Add the curry powder or paste, coriander and cream and simmer gently until reduced by a third. When the pork is cooked, slice the fillets and pour sauce over.

Ingredients

2 tbsp oil
4 x 6 oz (175g) pork fillets, patted dry on kitchen paper
salt and pepper
1 tsp crushed coriander seeds (optional)
3 tsp curry powder **or** paste
1 tsp ground coriander
8 fl oz (225ml) double cream

LAMB
with Fresh Minted Barley

Ingredients

6 oz (175g) pearl barley
2 pints (1.25 litres) stock
1½ lb (700g) lamb, neck fillet
  or leg steaks
2 tsp oil
3-4 leeks, washed and sliced
3-4 carrots, cut into ½" (1cm)
  slices
juice and finely grated zest of
  1 lemon
salt and pepper to taste
2 tbsp chopped parsley
2 tbsp chopped mint
extra parsley to garnish

Method

First prepare the barley which can be done several hours in advance. Rinse the barley and place in a saucepan with 1 pint (600ml) of the stock. Bring to the boil and simmer for 30 minutes, when most of the stock will have been absorbed. Reserve.

Remove any excess fat from the lamb fillet and using a very sharp knife, lightly score the surface on both sides. (Keeps meat flat when cooking).

Heat the oil in a frying pan and add the lamb. Cook over a medium heat until golden brown on both sides. Remove from the pan.

Off the heat, add the vegetables to the pan, the part-cooked pearl barley and the remaining 1 pint (600ml) stock. Return the pan to the heat and bring just to the boil.

Stir in the lemon juice and zest and then return the lamb to the pan, cover and simmer gently for 20 minutes, or until the barley is tender and has absorbed most of the stock. Lift out the lamb, cut into thin slices and arrange on warm plates.

Season the barley to taste and stir in the parsley and mint. Spoon onto the plates beside the lamb and serve immediately sprinkled with chopped parsley. Accompany with a side salad if liked.

HONG KONG PORK

Method

Heat 2 tablespoons of oil in a frying pan. Add the onion, pepper, garlic and water chestnuts (if available). Cook for 6-7 minutes until the onion is soft. Transfer vegetable mixture to a casserole.

Wipe the pan out and then heat again with a further 2 tablespoons of oil. Dust the pork with 2 dessertspoons of cornflour, and then brown the meat in the heated oil in 2 or 3 batches. Add the meat to the casserole.

Drain the syrup from the lychees into a jug and make up to 8 fl oz (250ml) if necessary with cold water. Place in a bowl followed by vinegar, sugar, ketchup, soy, salt and pepper and another dessertspoon of cornflour, blended with a little water.

Mix well, heat in a saucepan until boiling and pour over the pork and vegetables. Stir everything gently, cover and cook in the oven at 350°F/180°C/gas mark 4 for about 1 hour.

Test the pork for tenderness and when just about ready, stir in the lychees to fully heat through in the oven for a few more minutes.

Serve with rice or hot buttered noodles, plus another green vegetable if wished.

Ingredients

2-4 tbsp oil
1 large onion, chopped
1 large green pepper, deseeded and chopped
1 small can water chestnuts, sliced
1 clove garlic, crushed
1¼-1½ lb (600-700g) lean pork, diced
3 dsp cornflour
15 oz (425g) can lychees in syrup
2 tbsp wine vinegar
1 tbsp soft brown sugar
1 tbsp tomato ketchup
2 tbsp soy sauce
salt and pepper

TWO TERRIFIC CURRIES

MILD KHEEMA CURRY

Ingredients

2 tbsp vegetable oil **or** butter
1 large onion, finely chopped
2 cloves garlic, chopped
1½" (4cm) piece fresh root ginger, peeled and grated
1½ lb (700g) lean minced beef **or** lamb
3 tbsp natural yoghurt, mixed with 1 egg yolk
1 large tomato, peeled, deseeded and diced
2 tsp ground coriander
1 tsp ground cumin
1 tsp ground turmeric
¼ tsp cayenne pepper (can be omitted if required to suit children)
¼ tsp garam masala
2 tbsp tomato puree
1 tsp salt
8 oz (225g) peas, fresh **or** frozen
8 fl oz (225ml) water
1 tbsp finely chopped mint leaves

Method

Heat the oil or butter in a saucepan over a medium heat. Add the onion and cook, stirring until the onion is a pale gold colour. Then add the garlic and grated ginger and continue to cook, stirring for another minute.

Add the minced meat, stirring to break up any lumps, and continue cooking until the meat changes colour and begins to brown.

Next add the yoghurt, tomato, ground spices, tomato puree and salt to the pan. Stir everything together well, cooking for a further minute, and then turn the heat to low, cover the saucepan and cook gently for 10 minutes.

Uncover the pan, turn up the heat to medium and add the peas, water and mint and stir in. Bring to the boil, reduce the heat again, allowing the mixture to just bubble gently, and continue to cook until the peas are done and most of the liquid has evaporated. This dish should have a small quantity of thick gravy.

Turn onto a warmed serving dish and surround with boiled rice. Fried bread triangles are a traditional accompaniment.

MILD CURRIED PORK

Method

Place the pork into a bowl and sprinkle over the salt, turmeric and cayenne pepper. Stir through to coat the meat cubes and leave to stand for one hour.

Place the onion, ginger and garlic in the food processor or blender and process to make a smooth puree. Then heat the oil in a large pan over a medium heat add the puree, and fry, stirring until the moisture has evaporated from the onions (about 5 minutes).

Then add the marinaded pork cubes and stir. Continue to fry together for 5 minutes, scraping the base of the pan to prevent the spices sticking. Add the shrimp or anchovy paste, fish sauce, mango pickle, lemon juice and water.

Cover, reduce the heat to low and simmer gently for 1 hour, or until the meat is very tender. Uncover the pan occasionally to check the amount of liquid; adding up to 5 fl oz (150ml) more water if necessary. Stir in the mango slices, cover and cook for 2 more minutes.

Transfer to a heated serving dish or plates and accompany with boiled rice.

Ingredients

2 lb (900g) boneless lean pork, cut into 1½" (4cm) cubes
1 tsp salt
1 tsp ground turmeric
1 tsp cayenne pepper
2 onions, chopped
1-2" (2.5-4 cm) piece fresh root ginger, peeled and grated
4 cloves garlic, chopped
4 tbsp peanut oil
½ tsp shrimp paste **or** ½ tsp anchovy paste
1 tbsp nam pla (South Asian fish sauce - optional)
2 tbsp mango pickle (**not** chutney)
juice of 2 lemons
8 fl oz (225ml) water (plus a little more if necessary to prevent drying out during cooking)
1 large or 2 small mangoes, peeled, stoned and the flesh sliced or diced

MARVELLOUS MINCE

Ingredients

12 oz (350g) pasta shapes
oil
1 large onion, chopped
1½ lb (700g) minced beef
6 oz (175g) red **or** green
   pepper, cut into large dice
6 oz (175g) mushrooms,
   quartered or sliced
1 clove garlic, crushed
pinch of cayenne pepper
salt and pepper
for the white sauce:
1½ oz (40g) plain flour
1½ oz (40g) butter, cubed
1 pint (600ml) milk
salt and pepper
for the topping:
2 oz (50g) grated cheese
   (see note)

Method

Cook the pasta and drain well. Heat the oil in a pan and cook the onion until softened. Add the minced beef and cook until browned all over. Drain off any excess fat from the pan.

Add the chopped peppers, mushrooms, garlic, cayenne and salt and pepper. Mix everything together well and place in an ovenproof baking dish. Add the cooked pasta to the dish and mix thoroughly.

To make the white sauce simply put all the sauce ingredients into a saucepan over a medium heat and whisk continuously until the mixture boils and thickens. Then allow to simmer very gently for 5-6 minutes to 'cook' the flour, stirring frequently.

Pour the white sauce all over the dish and scatter the cheese over the top. Bake in the oven at 325°F/170°C/gas mark 3, uncovered, for 1 hour.

• Interesting mixtures of cheese could be: Mozzarella and Cheddar, Emmental and Parmesan – but you can always rely on Cheddar!

STOCKWOOD PARK PORK

Method

Dry the chops and season on both sides with some pepper.

Heat the oil in a pan and fry the pork until browned on both sides. Add the shallots with a little salt, cover and cook for 6-8 minutes. When the meat is done, remove to a serving dish and keep warm.

Mix the two mustards together and stir into the pan juices with the white wine, butter, mushrooms, tarragon and paprika. Stir to mix, and bring to the boil.

Allow to simmer for a couple of minutes, then stir in the cream. When hot and well blended serve over the pork.

Boiled new potatoes and any seasonal vegetable to accompany.

Ingredients

4 boneless loin pork chops
pepper
1 tbsp oil
1 tbsp finely chopped shallots
   or 1 tbsp finely chopped
   spring onions plus ½ clove
   crushed garlic
salt
2 tsp coarse-grain mustard
2 tsp Dijon mustard
4 fl oz (110ml) white wine
4 oz (110g) mushrooms,
   sliced or chopped
½ oz (15g) butter
1 tsp tarragon leaves
½ tsp paprika
5 fl oz (150ml) cream
finely chopped parsley

SPICY BEEF

Ingredients

1 lb (450g) lean minced beef
4 tbsp olive oil
1 large onion, chopped
1 green pepper, deseeded and
  chopped
1 clove garlic, crushed
1-2 tbsp chilli powder (to
  taste)
½ tsp curry powder
½ tsp paprika
1 bay leaf
2 tbsp wine vinegar
¾ pint (450ml) just boiled
  water *mixed with* 1 tbsp
  tomato puree
12 oz (350g) canned chopped
  tomatoes
12 oz (350g) cooked black eye
  or red kidney beans (canned
  or prepared from dried
  beans)
salt to taste

Method

Brown the beef in a large flameproof casserole or heavy saucepan with 2 tablespoons of olive oil, crumbling it with a fork until well cooked.

Make a space in the centre of the meat and add another tablespoon of the olive oil to the pan, followed by the onion, green pepper and garlic. Mix together with the beef and fry gently until the vegetables are tender.

Add chilli and curry powder, paprika, bay leaf, vinegar and water. Cover and simmer for 50 minutes, stirring several times, and if it gets too dry you can add a little more hot water.

After the 50 minutes, remove the bay leaf and add the tomatoes and beans and continue to cook for 15 minutes. The end result should be fairly thick and can now be seasoned with salt to taste.

Serve with warm pitta bread and if wished some grated cheddar cheese and greek yoghurt or soured cream.

A DISH OF PORK

Method

Preheat the oven to 325°F/170°C/gas mark 3. Trim and cut the spring onions into ½" (1cm) lengths. Thickly slice the baby sweetcorn and de-seed and dice the peppers.

Heat the oil in a pan and lightly brown the pork. Remove from the pan. Add the vegetables, garlic and ginger and stir-fry for 2 minutes.

Mix in the pineapple juice, vinegar, soy sauce, ketchup and sugar and then add the pork. Cover and simmer for 5 minutes, then transfer the pork mixture to a casserole dish, cover and cook in the oven for 1 hour.

Mix the cornflour with 1 tablespoon of cold water and stir into the pork, then cook for a further 30 minutes.

Serve with rice, pasta and fresh vegetables.

Ingredients

1 bunch spring onions
4 oz (110g) baby sweetcorns, thickly sliced
1 small red pepper
1 small green pepper
1 tbsp vegetable oil
1 lb (450g) boneless pork, cubed
1 clove garlic, crushed
1 tsp grated root ginger
½ pint (300ml) pineapple juice
4 tbsp cider vinegar
3 tbsp soy sauce
3 tbsp tomato ketchup
1 tbsp soft brown sugar
1 tbsp cornflour

ITALIAN STYLE BEEFBURGERS
with Herb, Cheese and Tomato Sauce

Ingredients
(serves 4-5)
for the sauce:
1 medium onion, chopped
2 cloves garlic, crushed
2 tbsp olive oil
2 tbsp fresh chopped parsley
1 tsp dried tarragon
2 x 14 oz (400g) cans chopped
  tomatoes
2 tbsp tomato puree
¼ pint (150ml) chicken stock
small glass red wine
2 tsp sugar
1 oz (25g) Parmesan cheese,
  freshly grated
½ tsp salt
1 dsp fresh marjoram **or**
  ½ tsp dried marjoram
for the meatballs:
2 slices white bread, soaked in
  2 tbsp water
1lb (450g) lean beef mince (or
  lamb)
2 large eggs, lightly beaten
1 oz (25g) Parmesan cheese,
  freshly grated
2 tbsp fresh chopped parsley
1 clove garlic, crushed
2 tsp fresh marjoram **or** 1 tsp
  dried marjoram
½ tsp salt
pepper
2 tbsp olive oil

Method
To make the sauce: in a heavy saucepan cook the onion and garlic in the oil over a low heat, stirring for 2 minutes.

Then add the parsley, tarragon, tomatoes, tomato puree, stock, wine, sugar, Parmesan, salt and the marjoram. Simmer the sauce, stirring occasionally for 30 minutes.

Meanwhile, to make the meatballs, break the bread into pieces and place in a bowl, add the water and allow to soak.

In a large bowl combine the squeezed out bread with the beef, eggs, Parmesan, parsley, garlic, marjoram and salt and pepper. Mix well and then form the mixture into 10 meatballs, and flatten slightly.

In a large pan brown the burgers in the oil over a high heat, turning often. Transfer the meatballs to the sauce with a slotted spoon and simmer the mixture, stirring occasionally for 30 minutes.

Ideal with mashed potatoes and any green vegetable.

FIFTY-FIFTY MOUSSAKA

Method

Cook the lentils according to packet instructions with the bay leaf, and reserve.

Heat the oil in a large pan and gently cook the onion and garlic until soft. Stir in the meat and continue cooking until lightly browned. Add the tomatoes, wine, tomato puree and the lentils. Then add the herbs, cinnamon and seasoning to taste.

Cover and simmer gently for about 25 minutes until nicely cooked and thickened. Transfer to an ovenproof dish.

Meanwhile, during the meat cooking time (or even earlier in the day if wished) slice the aubergines, brush with oil and grill or fry until lightly browned and soft. Arrange the slices on top of the meat mixture.

To make the topping place the butter, oil, flour, nutmeg and milk in a saucepan and cook gently, whisking continuously until it boils and thickens. Allow to simmer very gently for a few minutes then turn off the heat. Stir in seasoning to taste, the egg yolk and the cheeses.

The topping can also be made in advance but it does get thicker when cool and will also need to be covered with buttered paper to prevent a thick skin.

Pour the sauce over the aubergines, top with a little more grated cheese if wished and bake at 200°C/400°F/gas mark 6 for about 20 minutes until heated through and lightly browned and bubbling on top.

Allow to stand for 10 minutes before serving. Salad and crusty bread would be an ideal partnership.

Ingredients

4 oz (100g) green lentils **or**
  1 x 15 oz (425g) can cooked green lentils
1 bay leaf
2 tbsp olive oil
1 large onion, chopped
1 or 2 cloves garlic, crushed
8 oz (225g) lean mince lamb (or beef)
15 oz (425g) can chopped tomatoes
¼ pint (150ml) red wine
1 tbsp tomato puree
1 tsp dried mixed herbs
½ tsp dried oregano
salt and pepper
¼ tsp cinnamon
oil for brushing
2 aubergines, thinly sliced (just before cooking)

for the topping:
1 oz (25g) butter
1 tbsp olive oil
2 oz (50g) plain flour
1 pint (600ml) milk
grated nutmeg
2 oz (50g) Cheddar cheese
1 tbsp parmesan cheese
1 egg yolk

WINTER MINCE

Ingredients

2 tbsp oil
1 onion, sliced
5 oz (150g) sliced celery
1-2 cloves garlic, crushed
2-3 oz (50-75g) diced bacon
1 lb (450g) lean minced beef
(or lamb)
1 tbsp plain flour
2 tbsp mild curry powder (see
note)
1 tsp fresh ginger, grated **or**
½ tsp ground ginger
1 dsp tomato puree
½ pint (300ml) light stock
¼ pint (150ml) natural
yoghurt *mixed with* 1 level tsp
cornflour (see note)
6 tomatoes, peeled, deseeded
and quartered **or** 8 oz
(225g) canned chopped
tomatoes
8 oz (225g) cucumber, skin on,
diced
1 oz (25g) flaked almonds
1½ oz (40g) butter
paprika
chopped parsley

Method

In a flameproof casserole, heat the oil and gently fry the onions and celery until soft and shiny, then add the garlic and bacon and stir-fry for 1 minute.

Add the mince and brown completely, then stir in the flour, curry powder, ginger and tomato puree. Follow these with the stock, mixing in well and then stir through the yoghurt mixture before finally adding the tomatoes.

Bring to the boil, cover and put into the oven at 375°F/190°C/gas mark 5 for about 45 minutes.

Lightly fry the cucumber in 1oz (25g) of butter and stir into the casserole for the last 10 minutes of cooking time.

Lightly brown the almonds in the remaining butter and sprinkle with paprika. Use to garnish the dish, with a little chopped parsley (or coriander). Serve with rice or pasta.

• The curry powder I used in this dish was Sharwoods Malaysian which gives a subtle and delicately spiced flavour.

• Greek style yoghurt, I find, is better for cooking and gives a creamier finish to the sauce.

HONEY BLOSSOM PORK

Method

In a bowl mix together the oil, sherry, honey, vinegar and soy sauce. Season well with pepper. Marinate the pork in this mixture for at least 2 hours, turning from time to time.

In a pan heat 1 tablespoon of oil and then gently fry the onion, carrot, pepper and mushrooms. Place these in an ovenproof casserole. Drain the pork, pat dry and then brown in the remaining oil.

Transfer to the casserole and add the marinade, stock, seasoning and remaining sauce. Cover and cook in the oven at 350°F/180°C/gas mark 4 for 60-75 minutes.

Test the pork after 1 hour for tenderness. Then add the beansprouts to the casserole and mix in the cornflour. If including the waterchestnuts or bamboo shoots they should be added at this stage.

Return to the oven to cook for another 10 minutes, or until the pork is completely tender. Taste and adjust the seasoning. Serve with rice or noodles.

Ingredients

2 tbsp oil
2 tbsp sherry
2 tbsp honey
3 tbsp vinegar
2 tbsp soy sauce
pepper
1½ lb (700g) pork, cubed
2 tbsp oil
1 onion, chopped
3 carrots, peeled and diced
1 green pepper, deseeded and diced
4 oz (110g) mushrooms, halved or quartered according to size
¾ pint (450ml) stock
1 tbsp soy sauce
8 oz (225g) bean sprouts
1 small can of water chestnuts, sliced **or** bamboo shoots (optional)
1 tbsp cornflour, mixed with a little cold water

BRAISED LOIN OF PORK

Ingredients
(serves 6)

2½ lb (1.25kg) loin of pork,
  boned and skin removed
1 clove garlic, crushed
salt and pepper
4 tbsp olive or vegetable oil
1 tsp dried oregano
2 tbsp sesame seeds
1 large onion, chopped
6 oz (175g) cabbage, shredded
12 oz (350g) potatoes, peeled
  and diced
8 oz (225g) parsnips, peeled
  and diced
1 tsp chopped fresh thyme
1 tsp chopped fresh sage
1 pint (500ml) cider
2 tbsp fresh orange juice
1 tbsp soy sauce
¼ pint (150ml) single or
  double cream
2 tbsp finely chopped parsley

Method

Place the pork in a flameproof casserole dish. Score the fat with a sharp knife and rub it with the garlic. Season with salt and pepper, pour over 2 tablespoons of oil followed by oregano and sesame seeds. Place in the oven to roast at 425°F/220°C/gas mark 7 for 20 minutes.

Remove the pork from the oven and surround the meat with the prepared onion, cabbage, potatoes and parsnips. Season with salt and pepper and sprinkle over the thyme and sage and pour in enough cider to come halfway up the vegetables.

Add the orange juice, remaining oil and soy sauce. Cover with two layers of foil, then the casserole lid and cook in the oven at 350°F/180°C/gas mark 4 for 1 hour 30 minutes, removing the foil for the last 15 minutes of cooking time.

When cooked, remove the meat to a warm place. Place the flameproof casserole on the hob and allow to simmer gently while thickening lightly with 1 dessertspoon of cornflour or arrowroot mixed in a little water and added to the sauce. Next add cream and finely chopped parsley and stir in well.

To serve, place vegetables on the plate and top with the thinly sliced pork.

SAUTÉED LAMB
with Fresh Herb Dressing, Diced Minted Pears and Mashed Potato with Caramelised Onions and Pine Nuts

Method

Lightly beat the lamb slices between cling film with a rolling pin then brush with oil on both sides and season with pepper. Cover and keep at room temperature.

Put the potatoes to boil until tender. Meanwhile, stir fry the onions in the oil until soft and nicely browned. Keep warm (or re-heat just before use).

Drain and dice the pears and mix in the mint. Reserve in a bowl.

Mash the potatoes then beat in the butter, milk and seasoning until light and fluffy. Keep warm or just before serving reheat with a little extra milk or even cream.

Toast the pine nuts in a small dry pan, tossing frequently until tinged with brown. Then reserve in a small dish.

Now it's time to cook the lamb. Heat a dry heavy pan then add the slices (in two batches if necessary). Continue cooking until they have almost reached the desired degree. Add salt to taste.

Turn off the heat and after 1 minute add the butter and herbs which are mixed through the lamb pieces. Cover while you get the potato, pears, onion and pine nuts.

Serve on individual plates or one large dish as follows: potato topped with the onions and nuts; pears on the side; and the herb-dressed lamb in a simple pile. Another green vegetable is recommended or even a seasonal salad.

Ingredients
(serves 4)

1-1¼ lb (500-600g) lean lamb slices in 2 inch pieces (approx)

1-2 tbsp oil

pepper

1½ lb (750g) peeled potatoes

2 onions peeled and sliced thinly

3 tbsp oil (olive if possible)

1 tin of pear halves

1 heaped tbsp freshly snipped mint leaves

1-2 tbsp butter

4 tbsp milk

salt and pepper

2 tbsp pine nuts

salt

2-3 oz butter

2-3 oz chopped mixed herbs: parsley, marjoram, thyme, chives, tarragon etc (as available)

BOBOTIE

Ingredients

2 lb (900g) minced lamb (or
   beef)
a little oil
2 onions, chopped
2 dessert apples, peeled and
   chopped
2 cloves garlic, crushed
1 tbsp oil
2 oz (50g) butter
2 dsp curry powder
2 oz (50g) flaked almonds
3 oz (75g) raisins
1 tsp mixed dried herbs
1 tbsp chutney
juice of ½ lemon
1 tbsp wine vinegar
salt and pepper
3 slices white bread (crusts
   removed)
1 pint (600ml) milk
3 eggs
1 tbsp flour

Method

Preheat the oven to 375°F/190°C/gas mark 5.
First, in a little oil, gently cook the lamb mince (in
batches if necessary) until the meat has just
changed colour (do not overbrown) and place the
meat in a large mixing bowl

Next fry the onion, apples and garlic together
gently in the oil and butter.

Add the curry powder and continue cooking for
a minute or two and then add this mixture to the
lamb in the bowl, followed by the almonds, raisins,
herbs, chutney, lemon juice, vinegar and salt and
pepper to taste. Mix together well.

In another bowl soak the white bread in the milk
and then squeeze it out reserving the milk. Mix
the bread and one egg into the meat mixture and
spread it all in a well-buttered pie dish or low
casserole.

Beat the remaining milk with the two remaining
eggs and the flour and pour this all over the meat.
Bake in the oven for about 1 hour, when the
mixture should be set and the top browned.

Serve with boiled rice and a mixed leaf salad
dressed as you prefer.

PORK FILLET
with Mushrooms and Peppers

Method

Heat the oil or lard and then quickly fry the meat slices for 2 minutes on each side. Remove and keep to one side.

Into the same pan put the peppers and cook for a few minutes, then add the garlic, mushrooms and the chilli and stir-fry together for 5 minutes.

Add the wine and the vinegar, stir well then reduce the heat and continue to fry for 6-7 minutes.

Return the meat to the pan with its juices, stir through the peppers to heat, taste for seasoning and then serve at once with fried potatoes.

Ingredients

1¼ lb (600g) pork fillet, cut across into slices

2 tbsp oil **or** 2 oz (50g) pork lard

12 oz (350g) peppers, deseeded and cut into ½" (1cm) pieces

2 cloves garlic, sliced

10 oz (275g) mushrooms, sliced (any preferred kind or a mixture as available)

1 small chilli pepper, deseeded and cut into rings

3 tbsp white wine

1 tbsp white wine vinegar

salt and pepper

finely chopped parsley **or** coriander leaves to garnish

SPICED STEAK

Method

Combine the white pepper, cayenne pepper, allspice and cumin in a small bowl.

Spread the steaks on a baking sheet or tray. With your fingers, rub the spice mixture into the beef and brush with oil.

Grill, barbecue or dry pan fry as required.

Ingredients

4 grilling steaks (any kind)

½ tsp ground white pepper

¼ tsp cayenne pepper

½ tsp ground allspice

½ tsp ground cumin

VARIETY SPICE

Ingredients

1 lb (450g) lamb **or** chicken livers, cut into bite-sized pieces
2 onions, thinly sliced
2 cloves garlic, finely chopped
1½ oz (40g) butter
2 tbsp oil
1 or more red or green chillies, finely chopped **or** ½ tsp dried chilli
1 tsp freshly grated root ginger
1 tbsp finely chopped coriander leaves, **or** freeze dried coriander
1 tsp ground cumin
½ tsp turmeric
½ tsp pepper
½ tsp salt, **or** to taste
2 oz (50g) creamed coconut, grated
½ pint (300ml) chicken stock

Method

Sauté the onions and garlic in butter and oil until soft.

Add chilli, spices and seasonings and stir well to blend. Then add the liver and stir for 3 minutes. Stir in the coconut and stock and then simmer, uncovered, for 8-10 minutes until the liver is cooked.

Serve over plain rice with accompaniments such as chutney, sieved egg yolk and chopped egg white, chopped peanuts, chopped spring onions, cucumber and red pepper.

Garnish with chopped coriander or parsley.

POULTRY

BAKED TURKEY STEAKS

Method

Preheat the oven to 350°F/180°C/gas mark 4. Put each turkey steak between two pieces of greaseproof paper or foil and beat with a meat hammer or rolling pin to flatten slightly. Season the turkey with salt and pepper.

In a pan heat the oil and butter together. Add the turkey steaks and quickly seal. Transfer the turkey with the pan juices to a shallow ovenproof dish. Sprinkle the herbs, lemon juice and honey over the turkey. Cover and bake for 25 minutes.

Arrange the turkey on a warmed serving plate, top with lemon slices which have been dipped into chopped parsley. Serve immediately with cooking juices and any favourite seasonal vegetables.

Ingredients

4 x 6 oz (175g) turkey breast
  steaks
1 tbsp oil
1 oz (25g) butter
1 tbsp chopped mint
1 tbsp chopped thyme **or**
  1 tsp dried thyme
2 tbsp lemon juice
2 tbsp honey
4 slices lemon
1 tbsp finely chopped parsley
salt and pepper

CHICKEN BERAS

Ingredients
(serves 4)
8 chicken pieces
salt and pepper
8 oz (225g) long-grain rice
2 tbsp olive oil
2 cloves garlic, crushed
1" (2½cm) piece fresh root
  ginger, finely grated
1 generous tbsp soy sauce
1 generous tbsp plum **or**
  oyster sauce
1 tsp honey
1 tsp caster sugar
¼ tsp cinnamon
¼ tsp powdered cloves **or**
  nutmeg
Accompaniments:
(use all or any available)
1 large onion, finely sliced and
  fried until brown
chilli sauce
chopped hard-boiled egg
diced cucumber
diced deseeded tomato
finely grated carrot
For garnish:
finely sliced spring onions and
  freshly chopped parsley **or**
  coriander leaves

Method
Sprinkle salt and pepper over the chicken pieces and steam or poach in stock until fully cooked (about 25 minutes). Remove and keep warm.

Cook the rice according to packet instructions and meanwhile in a small bowl mix together the soy sauce, plum sauce, honey, caster sugar, salt and pepper, cinnamon and cloves.

Heat the oil in a large pan or wok and stir-fry the garlic and ginger for 6 seconds quickly followed by the soy sauce mixture. When the pan contents are hot, add the chicken pieces, turning to coat and fully heat through.

When everything is ready, serve the chicken on the rice, garnished with the fried onion and other accompaniments, sprinkling the spring onion and parsley mixture over the chicken for the finishing touch.

FRAGRANT SPICED CHICKEN

Method

Heat the oil in a large saucepan or flameproof casserole and brown the chicken a few pieces at a time, until they are golden brown on both sides. Remove with a slotted spoon and place on kitchen paper to one side.

Reduce the heat and add the onion and garlic and cook together until just beginning to brown. Add the spices and poppy seeds followed by the salt, creamed coconut and chilli. Cook, stirring everything together well for another minute.

Add the tomatoes and cook for 3-4 minutes before returning all the chicken to the pan, along with 8 fl oz (225ml) water. Bring to the boil, cover and simmer gently for about 25 minutes, until the chicken is tender. Stir once during the cooking time.

Then add the cream, simmer for 2 minutes, adjust salt to taste and then serve, garnished with fresh coriander or parsley and lemon wedges.

Boiled rice to accompany plus chutney, Indian bread etc as available or liked.

Ingredients

3 tbsp oil

1½ lb (700g) skinless chicken breast fillets **or** boneless thighs

4oz (110g) onion, finely chopped

3 cloves garlic, finely chopped

1 heaped tsp ground cumin

2 tsp ground coriander

½ tsp ground turmeric

1 tsp ground paprika

1 tsp mild curry powder

1 tsp poppy seeds

1 tsp salt

2 oz (50g) creamed coconut, grated

1 small green chilli pepper, deseeded and finely chopped

6 oz (175g) tomatoes, skinned, deseeded and chopped

4-5 tbsp double cream

fresh coriander **or** parsley and lemon wedges to garnish

COUNTRY DUCKLING

Ingredients

4 duckling leg quarters **or** leg portions
salt and pepper
1 onion, finely sliced
2 oz (50g) butter **or** duck fat
2 lbs (1kg) red cabbage, cored and finely shredded
1 oz (25g) dark brown sugar
1 tbsp redcurrant jelly
2 tbsp port
1 Cox's apple, quartered and sliced
juice of half lemon
caraway seeds (optional)

Method

Prick the duck legs, sprinkle with salt and place on a rack in a roasting tin. Roast in preheated oven at 400°F/200°C/gas mark 6 for 40 minutes until golden.

Meanwhile blanch the red cabbage to improve the colour of the finished dish. Place the cabbage in a colander in the sink and pour over boiling water, or blanch for 1 minute only in a large pan of boiling water. Drain well before using.

Cook the onion in the melted fat in a heavy based pan for a few minutes until softened. Add the red cabbage and toss well, then add the sugar, redcurrant jelly, port and seasoning to taste. Cover and cook gently for 20 minutes.

Add the apple slices, lemon juice and if liked, a few caraway seeds. Turn into an ovenproof casserole dish and place the browned duckling legs on the top.

Cover and cook in the oven at 350°F/180°C/gas mark 4 for a further 1 hour until the duckling is tender. Remove the cover for the last 15 minutes of cooking time.

Potatoes, either plain boiled, crisp fried or creamy mashed and a green salad make ideal accompaniments.

DUCK FILLETS
on Savoury Rice

Method

Season the breast fillets and arrange, skin side up, in a baking tin. Roast in a preheated oven at 400°F/200°C/gas mark 6 for 30-35 minutes. Meanwhile prepare the rice.

Heat the duck dripping in a wok or large frying pan and add the onion and fry for 2-3 minutes. Add the garlic, celery and mushroooms, stirring for 2-3 minutes.

Stir in the prepared rice and lemon rind and season well. Stir everything over a brisk heat until thoroughly reheated. Remove from the heat and stir in the chopped watercress.

Spoon the rice into 2 rows on a hot serving dish. Cut the breast fillets diagonally, across the grain, into thin slices. Arrange over the rice and garnish with twists of lemon. Serve sauce separately.

Ingredients

4 duck breast fillets
6 oz (175g) long-grain **or** brown rice, boiled, drained and cooled
2 tbsp duck dripping
1 large onion, finely chopped
1 clove garlic, crushed
2 sticks celery, finely chopped
4 oz (110g) button mushrooms, quartered
finely grated rind of 1 lemon
salt and pepper
1 bunch watercress, trimmed and chopped
to garnish:
twists of lemon
a wine sauce or gravy

CHICKEN STIR-FRY

Ingredients
(serves 2-3)

1 orange
2 tsp cornflour
2 tbsp soy sauce
1 medium bulb of fennel **or**
   3 sticks celery, chopped
1 small red pepper
1 small yellow pepper
6 spring onions
8 water chestnuts (optional)
2 chicken breasts, skinned and
   boneless
1 tbsp oil
salt and pepper
1 tbsp finely chopped parsley

Method

Grate the zest from the orange and reserve. Squeeze the juice into a small bowl. Whisk in the cornflour and soy sauce and leave to one side.

Trim the base and top of the fennel and cut in halves. Cut each half into thin slices. Halve both the red and yellow peppers, discarding the stem, pith and seeds. Cut into thin slices. Trim the spring onions and cut diagonally into ½" (1cm) slices. Slice the water chestnuts.

Cut the chicken breasts into thin slices. Heat the oil in the pan, add the chicken and cook over a medium-high heat until beginning to brown, stirring constantly.

Add all the vegetables and continue to cook, stirring constantly, until the vegetables are just soft. Pour over the orange juice and cornflour mixture and cook, still stirring until the chicken and vegetables are coated with the glaze. Season to taste with salt and pepper.

Spoon the stir-fry onto warmed plates. Sprinkle over the orange zest and chopped parsley. Serve immediately with rice or noodles.

PING PONG CHICKEN

Method

Cut the chicken into bite-sized pieces and place in a bowl. Add the salt, lightly beaten egg white and the cornflour, then mix to coat the chicken pieces.

Heat about 2" (5cm) of oil in a wok or pan and fry the chicken pieces, a few at a time, for about 3-4 minutes for each batch, until browned. Don't overcrowd them otherwise they will stick together. Remove with a slotted spoon to a heatproof dish lined with kitchen paper. Keep warm while you make the sauce.

In a pan fry the onion and garlic in the oil until soft (see note below). Add the stock followed by the vinegar, sugar, soy sauce, tomato puree and sherry, and mix well. Blend the cornflour to a paste with the water and stir in. Cook for 1 minute, taste for seasoning and add the chilli sauce if wished.

Arrange the chicken pieces on a serving dish or plate and pour over the sauce. Rice and salad make a good accompaniment.

• The onion and garlic can be pre-fried if wished to avoid delay. Simply re-heat in the saucepan and continue with the recipe.

Ingredients

2 chicken breasts, skinned and boned
¼ tsp salt
1 egg white, lightly beaten
1½ tbsp cornflour
oil

for the sauce:

1 onion, finely chopped
1 clove garlic, crushed
1 tbsp oil
3 fl oz (75ml) chicken stock
1½ tbsp wine vinegar
1½ tbsp sugar
1½ tbsp soy sauce
2 tsp tomato puree
2 tbsp sherry
1 tbsp cornflour
4 tbsp water
salt and pepper
1 tsp chilli sauce (optional)

MIDSUMMER TURKEY CASSEROLE

Ingredients

1½ lb (700g) turkey meat, light, dark or mixed, cut into cubes

2 oz (50g) butter **or** 2 tbsp oil

4 oz (110g) celery, cut into 1" (2.5 cm) sticks

4 oz (110g) carrots, cut into small chunks

12 spring onion bulbs with just a little green part

2 dsp plain flour

½ pint (300 ml) chicken stock

2 tbsp lemon juice

salt and pepper

6-8 oz (175-225g) button mushrooms or 6-8 oz (175-225g) closed cup mushrooms, trimmed and halved

8 oz (225g) broad beans, frozen or canned

2 egg yolks

3 fl oz (75ml) double cream

2 tsp chopped tarragon

chopped parsley

Method

Heat the butter or oil in a flameproof casserole over a low heat. Add the cubes of turkey in batches and cook gently, turning constantly until just coloured, but not browned. Remove the turkey with a slotted spoon and reserve.

Add the celery, carrots and spring onions to the casserole and cook gently until slightly softened. Sprinkle on the flour and stir until smooth. Still stirring pour in the stock and lemon juice and bring to a simmer. Season with salt and pepper and return the turkey to the casserole. Cover and cook at a very gentle simmer for about 30 minutes.

Then stir in the mushrooms and broad beans. Return gently to simmering point, cover and cook for a further 20 minutes or so until the turkey is done and the vegetables are cooked.

In a small bowl beat the egg yolks with the cream and tarragon. Carefully stir in a few spoonfuls of the casserole liquid, then slowly pour the contents of the bowl into the casserole stirring all the time. Cook very gently for a few minutes more without boiling. Check seasoning and serve at once sprinkled with finely chopped parsley.

Boiled rice, noodles, boiled or mashed potatoes together with a green vegetable would make the ideal accompaniment.

HOLIDAY CHICKEN

Method

Examine the chicken pieces and trim off any extra fat from the edge of the skin. Heat 1 tablespoon of oil and 1 oz (25g) butter in a large pan and then brown the chicken all over.

Spoon or carefully pour off nearly all the browning juices and then season the chicken in the pan with salt and pepper. Add the chicken stock to the pan with the soy sauce and cook partly covered over a moderate heat for 20 minutes.

Meanwhile heat the remaining oil and butter in another pan, and over a high heat quickly sear the pineapple slices until they acquire a browned, caramelised surface on both sides. (A sprinkle of caster sugar during the process will assist with the browning).

When done, cut the pineapple into pieces and add to the chicken pan to continue cooking for an extra 10 minutes. If necessary, due to evaporation, a little extra chicken stock may be added at this stage. Finally correct the seasoning if needed and then serve with the combined garnish ingredients sprinkled over.

Sauté potatoes would go well with this dish and on the programme I served some steamed courgette slices dressed with seasoned melted butter and a few small capers.

Ingredients
(serves 4-6)

6 chicken legs (cut into 6 drumsticks and 6 thighs)
2 tbsp oil
2 oz (50g) butter
½ pint (300ml) good chicken stock (canned chicken consommé is ideal)
1-2 tsp soy sauce, naturally brewed Japanese is best
4 slices of pineapple, fresh if possible
2 tsp caster sugar

to garnish:

1 heaped tbsp chopped parsley
1 heaped tbsp browned flaked almonds
4 spring onions, finely shredded
1 tsp finely grated lime **or** lemon zest

TURKEY STEAKS
with Mint and Basil

Ingredients

3 oz (75g) butter
3 tbsp oil
4 x 5-6 oz (150-175g) turkey breast escalopes **or** steaks
6 oz (175g) mushrooms (cultivated or wild), cut into large pieces
4 shallots, peeled and finely chopped
½ tsp fresh thyme leaves **or** ¼ tsp dried thyme
1 clove garlic, peeled and halved
1 generous tbsp finely chopped parsley
2 tbsp lemon juice
salt and pepper to taste
6-10 basil leaves (depending on size)
6-10 mint leaves (depending on size)
1 tsp sherry vinegar **or** wine vinegar
4 fl oz (110ml) white wine
5 fl oz (150ml) chicken stock
8 fl oz (225ml) double cream
1 oz (25g) butter, diced and chilled

Method

Heat 1 oz (25g) butter with 1 tablespoon of oil and cook the turkey steaks over a moderate heat until fully cooked through but not overbrowned. Remove and keep warm in a covered dish.

Wipe out the pan and heat another tablespoon of oil with 1 oz (25g) of butter. Add half the shallots followed by the mushroom pieces and the thyme. Cook together until the shallots begin to turn golden, then add the garlic clove, followed by the lemon juice, parsley and seasoning to taste. Allow to reduce for a couple of minutes, then remove to a warm place (ideally a covered bowl).

Once more wipe out the pan and add the remaining butter and another tablespoon of oil. Gently fry the remaining shallots until soft and while they cook, roll up the basil and mint leaves together and quickly shred finely with a knife or kitchen scissors. Add them straight away to the pan followed by a dash of vinegar and the white wine. Bring to the boil and allow to reduce by about three-quarters.

Next add the stock and cream and reduce to a sauce consistency (until it coats the back of a spoon). Whisk in the diced butter pieces and check seasoning to taste.

To serve: Arrange the mushrooms in the centre of each warm plate. Place a turkey steak on top and divide the sauce over each portion. Garnish to taste with a sprig of mint or basil or even some finely chopped parsley. Accompany with any seasonal vegetable and simply boiled potatoes.

JAMAICA CHICKEN

Method

Put the first 9 ingredients in a shallow bowl and season with salt and pepper and leave for 1 hour to marinate.

Remove the chicken pieces, scrape off any marinade and dry the chicken pieces on kitchen paper. Reserve the marinade.

Heat the oil in a large frying pan and add the onion and fry until soft. Remove from the pan and add the chicken pieces. Fry until golden, then return the onion to the pan with the reserved marinade, white wine and hot pepper sauce.

Add enough water to just cover the chicken and bring to the boil and simmer, covered, for about 45 minutes, until the chicken is tender and fully cooked. If necessary reduce the sauce by removing the cover for the last few minutes of the cooking time.

Serve with rice and a salad.

Ingredients

4 chicken quarters, halved
3 cloves garlic, chopped
1 large bunch thyme **or** ½ tsp dried thyme
1 tsp chopped basil leaves
1 bay leaf
juice of 1 lemon
10 allspice berries, coarsely crushed **or** 1 tsp ground allspice
2 fresh red **or** green chillies, deseeded and finely shredded
2 large tomatoes, chopped
salt and pepper
3 tbsp oil
1 large onion, finely sliced
1 glass dry white wine
1 tsp West Indian hot pepper sauce

CHICKEN SATAY

Ingredients

1 lb (450g) skinless chicken
  breasts **or** thigh fillets
1 large onion, grated
2 tbsp lemon **or** lime juice
2 cloves garlic, crushed
2 tsp grated fresh ginger
2 tsp crushed chillies
3 fl oz (75ml) soy sauce
2 tbsp brown sugar
1 tbsp sesame oil
6 fl oz (175ml) coconut milk
4 oz (110g) crunchy peanut
  butter
2 tbsp toasted sesame seeds
bamboo skewers for grill or
  barbecue use

Method

Cut the chicken breasts into bite-sized pieces. In a bowl mix together the onion, lemon juice, garlic, ginger, crushed chillies, soy sauce, brown sugar and sesame oil. Pour this mixture all over the chicken pieces, and stir until the chicken is thoroughly coated. Leave to marinate for 1 hour in the refrigerator.

Meanwhile soak the bamboo skewers in cold water. Remove the chicken pieces from the marinade and thread onto soaked bamboo skewers (see note), leaving a portion of the skewer free for handling.

Barbecue over a preheated grill for about 6 minutes, turning until they are nicely browned. Alternatively simply pan-fry the diced chicken until fully cooked. Brush with a little extra oil if necessary.

Pour the remaining marinade into a pan and place on the edge of the barbecue or hob. Add the coconut milk and peanut butter, stir until the mixture boils and thickens.

Serve satays on a dish, sprinkling them with sesame seeds. Accompany with boiled rice and serve with satay sauce.

• If wished the chicken may simply be pan-fried as demonstrated, but the skewers are particularly suited to grilling and barbecueing.

TURKEY MILANO

Method

Heat the oil and butter and gently stir fry the onion, celery, leeks and carrots until soft and shiny, then add the garlic and lemon strips, stir through and put into a casserole.

Coat the turkey in the flour seasoning and coriander mixed together. Heat the olive oil in the wiped out pan and lightly colour the turkey pieces all over, in batches, adding them to the casserole as you go.

Pour the wine into the hot pan and allow to boil and bubble for 4-5 minutes scraping up any bits over the pan (deglazing). When the wine is reduced by half add the stock then simmer for three minutes. Pour over the turkey and vegetables.

Next, swiftly add the chopped tomatoes, thyme, bay leaves, parsley, and basil leaves if available. Stir gently then cover and allow to simmer on the hob or into the oven at 180°C/350°F/gas mark 4 for 40-60 minutes until the turkey is fully cooked and tender.

Serve with rice and a salad plus a garnish of plain chopped parsley or parsley mixed with a teaspoon of finely grated lemon zest and a very finely chopped small garlic clove (called gremolada in Italy). A little finely chopped bacon and shallot mixture, fried until soft, can be used to garnish the rice with some finely grated Parmesan cheese.

Ingredients
(serves 4-5)

2 tbsp oil
2 oz (50g) butter
1 onion, finely chopped
2 carrots, finely chopped
2 leeks, finely chopped
2 sticks of celery, finely chopped
1 clove of garlic, finely chopped
2 strips of lemon peel
salt and pepper
3 oz (75g) plain flour
2 tbsp coriander seeds, roughly crushed
4 tbsp olive oil
1½ lbs (750g) turkey meat, diced into bite-sized pieces
8 fl oz (250ml) dry white wine
10 fl oz (300ml) chicken stock
1 tin chopped tomatoes with juice
½ tsp dried thyme
2 bay leaves
2 sprigs of parsley
4 fresh basil leaves torn (optional)
2 rashers of bacon
1 shallot

DIJON CHICKEN

Ingredients

(serves 4)

8 chicken pieces
1 tbsp oil
salt and pepper
1 clove garlic, crushed
1 bay leaf
1 dsp fresh chopped marjoram
  or 1 tsp dried marjoram
1 dsp fresh thyme leaves **or**
  1 tsp dried thyme
1 oz (25g) butter
6 fl oz (175ml) chicken stock
6 fl oz (175ml) dry white wine
8 small onions, peeled
12 whole baby carrots **or**
  6 oz (175g) carrot pieces
14 oz (400g) can artichoke
  hearts
2 dsp Dijon mustard
1 tbsp cornflour
finely chopped parsley

Method

Heat the oil in a large flameproof casserole and lightly brown the chicken pieces (see note). Then add a little salt and pepper, the garlic, bay leaf, marjoram, thyme, butter, chicken stock and wine. Bring to a gentle simmer, cover and cook for 35 minutes, stirring occasionally.

After the 35 minutes, add the onions, carrots and drained artichokes and cook covered for a further 10-15 minutes until all the vegetables are tender.

Transfer the chicken and vegetables to a warmed serving dish and keep warm in a very low oven. Stir the mustard into the cooking liquid and bring to the boil. Mix the cornflour with a little cold water, add to the pan and stir until just thickened.

Pour the sauce over the chicken and vegetables and serve immediately, garnished with chopped parsley.

• After the initial browning of the chicken, it may be necessary to spoon off some of the chicken fat.

MAPLE GLAZED CHICKEN

Method

In a jug combine the maple syrup, chilli/tomato sauce, onion, vinegar, mustard and Worcestershire sauce and pour over the chicken pieces in a baking dish or roasting tin.

Cover and marinate for 1-4 hours in the fridge, turning once or twice. Bake at 200°C/400°F/gas mark 6 until completely done, basting occasionally.

Garnish with chopped parsley and serve with salad leaves or a mixed bean salad with bread and booze to taste.

Ingredients
(serves 4)

2½ lbs (1kg) chicken pieces – wings, thighs or drumsticks

4 fl oz (125ml) pure maple syrup

5 dsp chilli sauce **or** tomato ketchup **or** any combination of the two to suit your taste

1 medium onion, chopped

2 tbsp cider **or** wine vinegar

2 tsp made mustard

1 tsp Worcestershire sauce

• If using chicken thighs or drumsticks, it's a good idea to slash in two places with a knife.

• Non onion eaters can substitute 6 oz finely diced celery sticks, perhaps adding a crushed clove of garlic if desired.

• The liquid in the baking dish can, if wished, be reduced to a syrupy sauce in a saucepan on the hob.

• The chicken can also be grilled or barbecued using the marinade to baste.

CHICKEN LIVER SAUCE

Ingredients
(serves 4)
½ lb (225g) chicken livers
2 tbsp chopped shallots **or** onion
3 tbsp olive oil
1 oz (25g) butter
1 clove garlic, finely chopped
1½ oz (40g) unsmoked bacon, diced
1½ tsp chopped sage
¼ lb (110g) lean minced beef
salt and pepper
1 tsp tomato puree *dissolved in* 4 tbsp dry white white vermouth, sherry or wine

Method
Rinse the chicken livers then pat dry and cut into small pieces.

Heat the oil and butter gently together and sauté the shallots until softened. Stir in the garlic followed by the bacon and sage. Stir-fry until the bacon is coloured, then add the minced beef and cook, breaking it down with your spatula until all pinkness is gone.

Season with salt and pepper, then stir in the chicken livers and cook until they have changed colour. Add the vermouth and tomato puree and stir in well, then allow to simmer for ten minutes.

Eat as soon as possible for maximum flavour enjoyment. This sauce is excellent with risotto (recipe on page 99) and is also good with pasta and as a savoury baked potato topping.

SPICY LIME CHICKEN

Ingredients
(serves 2-3)
2 skinned and boned chicken breasts cut into bite-sized pieces
1 tbsp oil
2 oz (50g) butter, softened
finely grated zest of 1 lime
juice of half the lime
salt and pepper
¼ tsp chilli flakes **or** powder (optional)

Method
Fry the chicken pieces in the oil until browned and cooked through.

Meanwhile, blend together in a small dish with a fork, the butter, lime, seasoning and chilli if liked. Just before serving the chicken, stir this delicious butter through or spoon some over each portion of chicken pieces.

Garnish with finely chopped parsley.

CHINESE CHICKEN CHOW

Method

Preheat the oven to 400°F/200°C/gas mark 6. First place the chicken in a pot with water, stock cube, parsley, bay leaf, onion and seasoning to taste. Bring to the boil and then simmer gently until cooked through. Cut the cooked chicken into bite-sized pieces and reserve 12 fl oz (450ml) of the cooking stock.

Heat a large pan or wok, add the oil followed by the cucumber, leeks, ginger (if using), mushrooms, green pepper, celery and bean sprouts. Stir-fry until partly cooked (3-4 minutes).

Transfer to a casserole, add the chicken pieces and mix together. In a bowl whisk together sherry and cornflour then, still whisking, add the soy sauce and reserved stock. Mix into the casserole and place in the oven, uncovered, for about 20 minutes, giving it a good stir after the first 10 minutes.

Cook the rice and then mix in the butter and red pepper. Serve chicken on the rice with a garnish of almonds and parsley.

Ingredients
(serves 4-6)

1¼ lb (570g) boneless chicken
water to cover
1 chicken stock cube
1 bay leaf
½ onion, peeled
salt and pepper
parsley sprigs with stalk
3 tbsp oil
10 oz (275g) cucumber, peeled and diced
2 leeks, cleaned and thinly sliced
1 tsp grated ginger root (optional)
7-8 oz (200-225g) closed cap **or** button mushrooms, trimmed and halved
2 sticks celery, finely sliced
1 green pepper, deseeded and diced
6 oz (175g) bean sprouts
3 tbsp dry sherry
2 dsp cornflour
3 tbsp soy sauce
12 fl oz (350ml) chicken stock

for the rice:
long-grain rice (allow 2 oz/50g per person)
knob of butter
½ red pepper, very finely diced
1 oz (25g) browned flaked almonds
1 tbsp chopped parsley

CORONATION CHICKEN

Ingredients

2¼-2½ lbs (1-1.25kg) skinless, boned, cold cooked chicken
1 tbsp oil
1 small onion, chopped
1 tbsp mild curry powder **or** paste
1 tbsp tomato puree
4 fl oz (110ml) red **or** white wine
1 bay leaf
juice of ½ lemon
4 canned apricot halves, finely chopped or mashed with a fork
½ pint (300ml) mayonnaise
4 fl oz (110ml) whipping cream
salt and pepper
watercress sprigs to garnish **and/or** cucumber strips or slices

Method

Cut the chicken into bite-sized dice. Heat the oil in a small pan and add the onion and cook for 3 minutes or until soft.

Add the curry spices, tomato puree, wine, bay leaf and lemon juice. Simmer, uncovered, for about 10 minutes until well reduced. Leave to cool completely.

Beat the cold curry sauce into the mayonnaise with the apricot puree. Lightly whip the cream and fold into the mixture. Season, add extra lemon juice if necessary.

Toss the chicken pieces in the sauce and transfer to a serving dish and garnish with watercress/cucumber. Can be lightly chilled before serving is wished.

FISH & SEAFOOD

FIRECRACKER PRAWNS

Method

In a bowl mix together all the dry ingredients. Then simply thread the prawns onto skewers (water-soaked if for grill or barbecue). Brush with oil and then sprinkle with the spice mix and cook.

• The amounts given here will do for up to 2 lbs (900g) prawns. Cooking time depends on size of prawns but hot and brief is best, particularly if the prawns are cooked defrosted.

• The amount of 'hotness' can be varied by the amount of cayenne pepper used. Mayonnaise flavoured with bottled barbecue sauce makes a good accompanying dip.

Ingredients

2 tsp black pepper
½ tsp salt
I tsp onion powder
I tsp dried chilli flakes
I tsp paprika
½ tsp cayenne pepper
I tsp dried oregano
I tsp thyme
I tsp garlic powder
2 lb (900g) large prawns
2 tbsp olive oil

HANDSOME HADDOCK

Ingredients

1½-2 lb (700-900g) smoked
haddock fillets
2 oz (50g) butter **or** margarine
2 oz (50g) plain flour
1 tsp mustard
salt and pepper
2 bay leaves
1 pint (600ml) milk
2 sticks celery, finely chopped

Method

Place the fish in a saucepan, cover with water and bring to the boil. Allow to cook for 5 minutes (see note below). Remove fish from the pan, drain and keep warm.

Place the butter, flour, mustard, salt and pepper, bay leaves and milk in a saucepan. Whisk continuously over a moderate heat while the sauce boils and thickens.

Allow to cook very gently with an occasional stir for 5 minutes then stir in the celery, chopped parsley, red pepper, tabasco and dill, if using. Add the eggs and allow to heat through.

Place the fish on a warmed serving dish and pour the sauce over. Decorate with sprigs of parsley and lemon wedges.

Serve with creamy mashed potatoes, or boiled potatoes plus a green vegetable.

• The fish can be cooked in plain water if wished but a simple court-bouillon will greatly enhance the flavour of the fish.

This can be made with 1¾ pints (1 litre) water, piece of onion, piece of carrot, 1 tablespoon lemon juice or white wine vinegar, salt and a few peppercorns simmered together for 30 minutes to infuse the flavours.

Simply slip the fillets into the hot 'broth' and cook for 5-8 minutes depending on the thickness of your fish.

SALMON FILLETS
with Bacon, Leeks and Juniper
on a Parsley Butter Sauce

Method

In a large frying pan or flameproof casserole heat the oil. Fry the bacon until it starts to become crisp at the edges, then add the leeks and stir-fry over a moderate heat until softened. Remove the bacon and leeks from the pan and keep warm.

Increase the heat and place the salmon skin side up in the hot pan, cook for 60 seconds to colour and then turn over. Place the bacon and leek mixture on top of the fish fillets, scatter over the juniper berries and cook for another minute.

Add the wine and allow to bubble up. Season and reduce to a simmer, cover and allow to cook for 3-6 minutes, depending on the thickness of the fillets, which should be just firm and lightly cooked.

Remove the fish carefully with its topping and place on a warmed serving dish or individual plates. Whisk the butter pieces in the remaining cooking juices in the pan. Stir in the parsley and then spoon onto the serving plate(s).

Squeeze over the lemon juice and serve with new potatoes and if wished green peas or mange tout.

Ingredients
(serves 4)

4 x 6 oz (175g) salmon fillet pieces
1 tbsp oil
4 oz (110g) streaky bacon, cut into pieces
8 oz (225g) leeks, mostly white part, sliced into ½" (1cm) pieces
8 juniper berries, crushed and chopped
1 glass medium dry white wine
2 oz (50g) butter, in small pieces
1 heaped tbsp finely chopped parsley
½ lemon
salt and pepper

FISH CASSEROLE

Ingredients

1-1¼ lb (450g-570g) haddock fillet, skinned

12 oz (350g) potatoes, peeled and cut into bite-size chunks

3 oz (75g) carrots, thinly sliced

4 oz (110g) onion, sliced into half circles

4 oz (110g) leeks (white part), sliced into thin rounds

4 oz (110g) mushrooms, trimmed and halved or quartered

2 oz (50g) butter

salt and pepper

½ tsp sugar

1 tbsp lemon juice

1 tbsp chopped parsley

4 fl oz (100ml) double cream

8 oz (225g) puff pastry

1 egg, beaten

Method

To make pastry circles, firstly preheat the oven to 425°F/220°C/gas mark 7.

Roll out the pastry and cut out four large rounds and place on a baking tray lined with non-stick baking parchment. Brush with beaten egg and bake in the oven for 10 minutes until risen and golden. Allow to cool slightly, then keep in a warm place or warm gently just before serving.

To make the casserole, cut the haddock across the fillet into ½ cm strips and reserve. Boil the potato pieces for 3 minutes, drain and reserve.

After preparing the rest of the vegetables melt the butter in a heavy pan or saucepan and cook the carrots, onions and leeks gently, stirring for about 5 minutes. Then add the mushrooms and sugar and continue cooking for a further 3 minutes, stirring constantly.

Transfer the mixture to a casserole or pie dish, season to taste and gently mix in the fish, potatoes, parsley cream and lemon juice. Cover (with double foil if no lid) and bake in the oven at above temperature for 20-25 minutes.

Split the pastry rounds completely in half. Serve the fish over the bottom half of pastry and place the top half on the fish.

Accompany with a salad or a further green vegetable. Garnish with extra parsley if wished.

SMOKED SALMON and AVOCADO PASTA SALAD

Method

Put all the dressing ingredients into a bowl and whisk together until smooth. Cook the pasta shells in plenty of boiling salted water until tender. Drain well, put into a bowl and toss in the dressing while still warm. Slice the smoked salmon into thin strips.

Halve the avocado and remove the stone. Scoop out the flesh with a melon scoop or peel and slice into bite-sized pieces. Finely chop the spring onions. Add the salmon, avocado, onions, radishes and prawns to the pasta and toss everything lightly together.

Transfer to a glass bowl or serving plate lined with crisp lettuce leaves. Sprinkle with the fresh herbs and pepper to taste.

• Other smoked fish, such as trout or mackerel, could replace the salmon.

Ingredients

for the salad:
8 oz (225g) pasta shells
salt
2 oz (50g) smoked salmon (see note)
1 avocado
6 spring onions
1 bunch radishes
4 oz (110g) peeled prawns
1 tbsp fresh chopped parsley
1 tsp fresh chopped dill
pepper
for the dressing:
3 tbsp lemon juice
2 tbsp salad oil
1 tbsp mayonnaise **or** Greek natural yoghurt
½ tsp French mustard
salt and pepper

TUNA PATÉ

Method

Put all the ingredients in a bowl, adding salt and pepper to taste, and beat together until well blended.

Spoon into a dish and chill before serving with hot buttered toast or biscuits. Also good as a sandwich filling.

Ingredients

7 oz (200g) can tuna fish, drained and flaked
2 hard-boiled eggs, chopped
8 oz (225g) cream cheese
2 tbsp chopped chives
2 tbsp chopped parsley
2 tbsp brandy (optional)
salt and pepper
1 tbsp lemon juice (optional)

SAUCY SALMON

Ingredients

(serves 2)

for the potatoes:
1 ¼ lb (600g) potatoes, peeled and cut into chunks
salt and pepper
1 oz (25g) butter
2 tbsp milk or 2 tbsp cream
1 tbsp finely chopped spring onion (optional)

for the sauce:
2 tbsp finely chopped shallots
2 tbsp white wine vinegar
1 tbsp fresh lemon juice
1 large egg yolk
2 tbsp drained capers
1 tsp snipped chives (if available)
3 tbsp unsalted butter, melted
2 lemon slices

for the vegetables:
4-6 oz (110-175g) sugar snap peas **or** mange tout
1 tbsp oil
1 tbsp finely diced red pepper
1 tsp soy sauce

for the fish:
2 or 4 pieces of skinned boneless salmon, weighing in total about 10 oz (275g) and lightly brushed with oil.

Method

Cook the potatoes in boiling salted water until tender, then drain and season to taste. Add the butter and milk or half the cream and mash well. Then add the remaining cream and beat with a wooden spoon until smooth. Stir through the spring onion if using and then keep warm to one side.

To make the sauce use a small saucepan and add the shallots, vinegar, lemon juice, 2 tablespoons of water and salt and pepper to taste. Simmer gently, stirring occasionally, until the liquid is reduced to a tablespoon.

Transfer the mixture to a bowl, add the egg yolk and the capers and chives and mix together with a fork. Then, still mixing, add the warm butter in a stream and blend the sauce until it has combined well. Season to taste with salt and pepper and then keep warm over a saucepan of hot water.

To cook the vegetables heat a wok or frying pan and add the oil. When quite hot add the peas. Stir-fry for 1-2 minutes then add the red pepper and soy sauce. Stir-fry again until tender crisp and reserve in a warm place.

Now cook the salmon. Place a dry (non-stick if possible) pan on the heat and when very hot sear the salmon on all sides before turning the heat down to medium and allowing to cook until just done, 2-4 minutes, depending on the thickness of the fish.

To serve: Place the mashed potato in the centre of the plate and put the salmon on top. Ladle or spoon the sauce over a third of the salmon allowing some to run down onto the plate.

Place the peas to one side and garnish with a little finely chopped parsley and a slice of lemon if wished.

OCEAN CASSOULET

Method

If using dried beans, soak overnight and simmer in fresh seasoned water until soft, and then reserve.

Soak the saffron in a few tablespoons of warm water. Place the fish with the pint of fresh water in a saucepan. Add the bay leaf and salt and pepper and cook gently until firm. Then remove the fish and cut into bite-sized pieces. Reserve the cooking liquor.

Fry the onion, celery and bacon together in the butter until softened, then add the ham followed by the cider or wine and the reserved cooking liquor.

Stir in the beans, herbs and spices and the saffron with its soaking water. Add the tomatoes and season with salt and pepper to taste. Bring everything to the boil and then cover and simmer gently for 20 minutes.

Add the fish chunks and a little extra liquid if necessary. Spoon into a shallow ovenproof dish and sprinkle the top with breadcrumbs and parsley. Cook in the oven at 375°F/190°C/gas mark 5 for 25 minutes until the topping is crispy.

• The saffron can be substituted with ¼ teaspoon of turmeric or omitted if wished.

• If using another fish instead of monkfish then leave the skin on and cut into pieces before poaching.

Ingredients

6 oz (175g) dried haricot beans **or** 15 oz (425g) can cannellini beans, drained

pinch of saffron threads **or** packet of saffron powder (see note below)

1 lb (450g) monkfish, filleted **or** other firm white fish (see note below)

1 pint (600ml) water **or** fish stock

1 bay leaf

1 onion, sliced

4 sticks celery, chopped

2 oz (50g) smoked bacon, diced

1 oz (25g) butter

4 oz (110g) cooked ham, diced

¼ pint (150ml) dry cider **or** white wine

½ tsp ground mace **or** ¼ tsp ground nutmeg

½ tsp dried or fresh thyme

½ tsp dried rosemary

4 tomatoes, skinned, deseeded and quartered

salt and pepper

for the topping:

6 tbsp fresh white breadcrumbs

3 tbsp chopped parsley

BAKED FISH FILLETS
with Herbed Citrus Dressing

Ingredients

for the baked fish:
2 tbsp finely chopped shallots
4 x 6-7 oz (175-200g) white
   fish fillets, **or** steaks (cod,
   haddock, halibut, turbot etc)
2 fl oz (50ml) white vermouth
   or dry white wine
2 fl oz (50ml) chicken stock
2 tsp fresh marjoram leaves
   or I tsp dried marjoram **or**
   oregano leaves
salt and pepper

for the citrus dressing:
I tsp Dijon mustard
4 fl oz (110ml) orange juice
I tsp grated lemon zest
I tbsp lemon juice
I tbsp extra virgin olive oil
2 spring onions, thinly sliced
2 tomatoes, peeled, deseeded
   and diced **or** I tbsp finely
   diced red pepper
I tbsp chopped parsley
salt and pepper to taste

Method

Preheat the oven to 450°F/230°C/gas mark 8. Sprinkle the shallots over the base of a shallow baking dish, just large enough to fit the fish in a single layer.

Place the fish on top, pour the vermouth and chicken stock over the fish and season with the herbs and salt and pepper. Bake in the oven, uncovered for 10-12 minutes, until just cooked.

Meanwhile prepare the citrus dressing. In a bowl whisk together the mustard, orange juice, lemon zest, lemon juice and olive oil until thoroughly blended. Stir in the spring onions and parsley. Season with salt and pepper.

Serve at once by transferring the fish to serving plates with a slotted spoon and pouring the citrus dressing over each portion. New boiled potatoes and a green vegetable to accompany.

• The citrus dressing is excellent with any kind of poached, grilled, baked or barbecued fish.

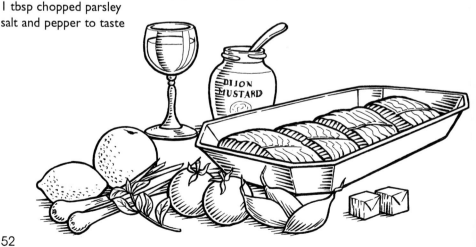

SALMON FLAN

Method

Scatter the flaked salmon pieces over the base of the blind-baked shortcrust flan case. Sprinkle over the grated Parmesan and diced Gruyère or Cheddar cheese followed by the dill.

In a bowl or jug whisk the eggs and extra yolks lightly together then add the cream, salt and pepper, cayenne and nutmeg. Whisk again to blend then carefully pour onto the salmon up to the rim of the pastry. (Any leftover mixture makes a wonderful addition to scrambled eggs).

Place the flan in the oven at 400°F/200°C/gas mark 6 for 10 minutes then reduce the oven temperature to 350°F/180°C/gas mark 4 and continue baking until slightly risen and browned (about 20-30 minutes).

Serve warm with salad and new potatoes. Also nice served cold but not chilled.

Ingredients

- 1 x 9"-10" (23-25.5cm) shortcrust flan case, baked blind for about 15 minutes at 400°F/200°C/gas mark 6.
- 8 oz (225g) cooked salmon, flaked (see recipe below)
- 1 tbsp freshly grated Parmesan cheese
- 1 tbsp diced Gruyère **or** Cheddar cheese
- 1 generous tsp fresh **or** dried dill weed
- 2 large eggs *plus* 2 egg yolks
- 10 fl oz (275ml) double cream
- salt and pepper to taste
- ¼ tsp cayenne pepper **or** 2 dashes Tabasco sauce
- ¼ tsp grated nutmeg

POACHING SALMON FILLETS OR STEAKS

Method

Place the salmon pieces in the cold liquid and bring slowly to a gentle boil whereupon turn off the heat and allow to rest for 2 minutes, then serve hot if that is the intention.

For cold salmon with mayonnaise etc keep the salmon in the cooking liquid until just before serving – this will keep it nice and moist.

Ingredients

- 1-1½ pints (600-900ml) cold water in a saucepan with:
- 2 tbsp white wine vinegar
- 2-3 onion slices
- 1 carrot, peeled and sliced
- 8 black peppercorns
- ½ tsp salt

To flake: After the cooking stage either leave it in the liquid as previously described or should time be pressing, remove the skin and the dark fat from the fillets and flake with a fork which will assist the cooling down period.

MUSSELS

Preparation

For absolute freshness eat on the day you buy, although you can keep them overnight submerged in water.

Wash the mussels well under running water and use a small vegetable knife to scrape off the barnacles and pull out the long threadlike strands (beard).

When thoroughly washed either cook straight away or if you're not ready to cook them leave submerged in water.

Throw away any mussels that have broken shells or any that remain open after being tapped sharply on the shell. Also discard any that remain closed after cooking.

MUSSEL SOUP

Ingredients

3½ pints (2 litres) fish, light chicken **or** vegetable stock
2 carrots
2 shallots
2 oz (50g) celery
2 tbsp olive oil
3 tomatoes
½ pint (300ml) dry white wine
saffron powder (optional)
5 lb (2.5kg) fresh mussels
8 fl oz (250ml) single cream

Method

Peel and dice the onions, carrots, shallots and celery. Heat the olive oil in a saucepan, add the vegetables and cook together gently until softened.

Peel the tomatoes, remove the seeds and chop the flesh. Add the tomatoes to the pan with half the wine, a pinch of saffron, if using, and the stock. Leave to cook for 20 minutes.

Scrub the mussels under running water and place them in another saucepan with the remaining wine and cook until they open (discard any that remain closed).

Remove the mussels from their shells and strain the liquor. Add the strained cooking liquor, the mussels and the cream to the soup and stir well.

Serve hot with crusty bread.

MOUCLAD

Method

Place the mussels and their accompanying ingredients, except for the milk, into a large saucepan. Bring to the boil, then cover and allow the mussels to steam open over a high heat, giving the saucepan a couple of vigorous shakes during the cooking time, which should be just a few minutes, depending on size.

Take out the mussels and then remove the empty half shell from each mussel and place the mussels in a bowl to keep warm under a folded tea towel. Strain the cooking juices (a piece of damp muslin or cheese cloth does the best job) into a jug and make up to 1 pint (600ml) with cold milk.

To make the mouclad sauce, soften the onion in the butter and then add the curry powder and nutmeg and cook gently for another 2-3 minutes. Stir in the mussel stock and bring to the boil, then reduce to a simmer and blend in the cream.

Arrange the mussels on a deep serving dish or individual bowls and pour the piping hot sauce over the mussels. Garnish with chopped parsley.

• The sauce can be lightly thickened if wished by the addition of 1 teaspoon of cornflour or arrowroot mixed with a little water.

Ingredients

(serves 3)
for the mussels:
3 lb (1kg 350g) prepared mussels
1 onion, chopped
2 sprigs parsley
2 quarters of lemon
2 sprigs of thyme **or** ½ tsp of thyme **or** ½ tsp dried thyme
1 bay leaf
½ pint (300ml) dry white wine
¼ pint (150ml) milk
for the sauce:
2oz (50g) butter
2 tbsp finely chopped onion **or** shallot
1 tsp curry powder
¼ tsp grated nutmeg
2 heaped tbsp crème fraîche **or** ¼ pint (150ml) double cream
2 tbsp finely chopped parsley

MOULES MARINIERE

Ingredients
(serves 4)
2oz (50g) butter **or** olive oil
1 onion, finely chopped
2 cloves garlic, crushed or
chopped
2 tbsp finely chopped parsley
½ pint (300ml) dry white wine
pepper
4 lb (2kg) of prepared mussels

Method
In a large saucepan gently heat the butter and soften the onion and garlic for a few minutes, then add the parsley, wine and pepper to taste, followed by the mussels.

Increase the heat and when it comes to the boil, cover and cook until the mussels have opened, giving the saucepan a couple of good shakes during this time (3-4 minutes should do it).

Serve in soup plates with fresh crusty bread.

BAKED GARLIC BUTTER MUSSELS

Ingredients
(enough for 40 mussels)
3 oz (75g) soft butter
3 cloves garlic, crushed
2 tbsp fresh white
breadcrumbs
2 tbsp finely chopped parsley
salt and pepper to taste

Method
Mix all the above ingredients together and use to stuff the steamed-open mussels, having discarded the empty shell of each mussel.

Place the stuffed mussels on a baking tray or ovenproof dish and bake in a very hot oven for 10 minutes.

A DISH OF FISH

Method

Gently heat together the butter and oil. Pour into a warmed baking dish and mix through the crushed garlic. Place the fish fillets in the dish and turn once to coat. If the skin is still on the fish make sure this is underneath.

Sprinkle a light dusting of paprika over the fish with some salt to taste. Spoon a teaspoon of soy sauce over each fillet. Mix together the spring onion and parsley and scatter all over the fish.

Top with flaked almonds and then cook in the oven at 350°F/180°C/gas mark 4 for about 25 minutes, giving the fish a baste with the cooking liquid half way through.

Serve hot with any combination of seasonal vegetables you fancy.

Ingredients
(serves 4)

1 oz (25g) butter
2 tbsp oil
2 cloves garlic, crushed
4 cod fillets (approx 6 oz/175g each) **or** any firm white fish
paprika
salt
1 tsp soy sauce
1 heaped tbsp finely chopped parsley
6 spring onions, finely chopped
1 oz (25g) flaked almonds

GLAZED SHALLOTS
and MUSHROOMS

Ingredients

2 tsp oil
8 oz (225g) mushrooms
8 oz (225g) shallots
2 tbsp honey
I tsp chopped fresh tarragon
   or ½ tsp dried tarragon

Method

Heat the oil in a non-stick frying pan over a medium heat. Add the mushrooms and sauté them until they are lightly browned, about 4 minutes. Transfer the mushrooms to a bowl.

Pour 8 fl oz (225ml) water into the pan and add the shallots, honey and tarragon. Partly cover the pan, bring the liquid to a simmer and cook the mixture until the shallots are translucent and only about 4 tablespoons of liquid remain, about 8-10 minutes.

Return the mushrooms to the pan and toss them with the shallots and the liquid until they are all coated with a syrupy glaze. Keep the glazed shallots and mushrooms warm until served.

POTATOES
with Walnut Dressing

Method

Peel the potatoes and bring to the boil in a pan of lightly salted water. Cook for 20 minutes until they are just tender. Drain and cut into chunks.

Heat the olive oil in a large frying pan and cook the garlic, basil, parsley, onion and lemon rind together for 2 minutes. Then add the potatoes and butter with salt and pepper to taste.

Cook over a moderate heat for 10 minutes, until golden on both sides.

Sprinkle with lemon juice and the ground walnuts. Toss lightly and serve.

Ingredients

2 lb (900g) waxy potatoes
4 tbsp olive oil
1 oz (25g) butter
2 cloves garlic, crushed
4 leaves fresh chopped basil
1 tbsp freshly chopped parsley
1 small onion, finely chopped
grated rind of 1 lemon
salt and pepper
juice of ½ lemon
1 oz (25g) walnuts, roughly ground in blender

COUNTRY BEAN and POTATO SALAD

Method

In a large bowl mix together the potatoes, French beans, cooked cannellini beans, onion, olives and capers.

Pour over the vinaigrette sauce and toss together well. Sprinkle with parsley and serve at room temperature.

• For the vinaigrette sauce, simply mix well together 2 fl oz (50ml) vinegar, 6 fl oz (175ml) oil, salt and pepper, adding 1 tablespoon chopped fresh mixed herbs (basil, parsley etc) or simply parsley.

Ingredients

1 lb (450g) new potatoes, boiled and diced
12 oz (350g) French beans, steamed and cut into 1" (2.5cm) lengths
20 oz (570g) of cooked cannellini beans, drained
1 small onion finely chopped **or** 1 large bunch of spring onions, chopped
2 oz (50g) black olives, stoned and sliced
1 tbsp capers
8 fl oz (250ml) vinaigrette sauce (see note)
1 tbsp freshly chopped parsley

MEDITERRANEAN POTATO CASSEROLE

Ingredients
5 fl oz (150ml) olive oil
2 medium onions, halved and finely sliced
2 cloves garlic, crushed
1 tbsp ground cumin
1 tbsp ground coriander
½ tsp cayenne pepper
2 lb (1kg) potatoes, peeled and cut into chunks
juice of 1½ lemons
½ pint (300ml) water
salt
1-2 tbsp chopped parsley

Method
Heat the olive oil in a saucepan and gently fry the onion until soft. Then add the garlic and stir for 30 seconds before mixing in the spices. Continue to stir for 1 minute, then add the potatoes and stir in well.

Pour over the lemon juice and water, adding salt to taste, then cover and cook for 20-30 minutes, stirring occasionally to prevent sticking.

Sprinkle the parsley over and serve accompanied by salad and plain Greek yoghurt.

SUMMER SOUP

Ingredients
½ large cucumber, chopped
12 oz (350g) courgetttes, chopped
1 large crisp lettuce, finely chopped
8 spring onions, chopped
4 tbsp oil
2 pints (1.15 litres) vegetable stock
½ pint (300ml) cream
juice of half a lemon
4 tbsp chopped dill **or** fennel

Method
Heat the oil in a large saucepan over a low heat and add the cucumber, courgettes and spring onion. Cover and cook gently together for about 10 minutes.

Pour in the stock and bring to the boil. Add half the chopped lettuce, cover and simmer for 15 minutes.

Liquidise the soup in a blender or food processor, and return to the saucepan. Stir in the cream and lemon juice.

Next stir in the remaining shredded lettuce and the chopped dill or fennel. Reheat gently, without boiling, and serve.

WELL-DRESSED SALAD

Method

Combine all the ingredients except the oil in a bowl, whisking lightly, then continue whisking as you pour in the olive oil. Store any unused dressing in a screw top jar.

• A good green salad is essential and even if it's only plain lettuce leaves this dressing will bring them magically to life. Salads should be lightly tossed with just enough dressing to coat the leaves at the very last minute before serving.

Ingredients

4 tbsp lemon juice
4 tbsp wine vinegar
½ tsp mustard powder
I tsp finely chopped red onion
I tsp fresh oregano **or** ½ tsp dried oregano
I tsp fresh thyme **or** ½ tsp dried thyme
2 cloves garlic, crushed
salt to taste
8 fl oz (250ml) extra-virgin olive oil

THREE BEAN SALAD

Method

Drain and rinse all the beans. Mix the dressing ingredients together thoroughly and combine with the beans. Allow to marinate for 2 hours.

Pile the beans into a serving dish and surround with the quartered tomatoes and lettuce leaves.

Ingredients

15 oz (425g) can chickpeas
15 oz (425g) can red kidney beans
15 oz (425g) can green flageolet beans
6-8 tomatoes, quartered
lettuce leaves
for the dressing:
¼ pint (150ml) olive **or** sunflower oil
4 tbsp white wine vinegar
2 tbsp chopped parsley
I tbsp chopped basil
I shallot, finely chopped
I clove garlic, finely crushed
salt and pepper

THE AUBERGINE COLLECTION

AUBERGINES with TOMATOES and FRESH HERBED CREAM

Ingredients

2 aubergines
2 fl oz (50ml) olive oil
8 ripe tomatoes, skinned and
 coarsely chopped
salt and pepper
2 oz (50g) butter
2 cloves garlic, chopped
1 tbsp finely chopped tarragon
1 tbsp finely chopped parsley
1 tbsp finely chopped chives
1 tbsp finely chopped basil
¾ pint (450ml) double cream

Method

Cut the aubergines into ½" (1cm) slices and fry on both sides in hot olive oil until golden. Drain on kitchen paper and leave to cool.

Heat the butter in a pan and season the tomatoes before stewing them in the butter for 5 minutes. Stir in the garlic and pour into a 2" (5cm) deep baking dish. Cover with overlapping slices of aubergine and season lightly with salt and pepper.

Stir the chopped herbs into the cream and pour over the aubergines. Bake in the oven at 375°F/190°C/gas mark 5 for 30 minutes, until bubbling and lightly browned.

An excellent accompaniment to grilled lamb chops.

AUBERGINES with SWEET CHILLI VINEGAR

Ingredients

1¼ lb (560g) aubergines
3 fl oz (75ml) groundnut oil
4 tbsp balsamic vinegar
2 tsp sugar
¾ tsp salt
3 tbsp finely shredded spring
 onions
½-1 tsp crushed dried red
 chilli

Method

Cut the aubergines into 1" (2.5cm) chunks. Heat the oil in a frying pan until hot and then add the aubergine chunks and fry until well browned. Drain on kitchen paper.

Add the vinegar, sugar and salt to the pan and bubble up. Add the spring onions to the pan and the chilli and then return the aubergines and stir carefully to mix.

Serve in a vegetable dish and if liked, decorate with coriander. Delicious on its own or with grilled and barbecued meat.

BAKED AUBERGINES
with FRESH PESTO

Method

Split the aubergines in half lengthways and with a sharp knife make a criss-cross pattern over the cut surfaces to a depth of about 1" (2.5 cm). Season with salt and pepper and brush the surfaces with a little olive oil.

Place in an ovenproof dish and bake in the oven at 425°F/220°C/gas mark 7 for 20-30 minutes, until very soft.

Meanwhile put the basil, garlic, pine kernels and a little salt and pepper into the food processor or blender, adding 3 fl oz (75ml) olive oil and blending to produce a loose-textured puree.

Pour into a bowl and stir in the grated Parmesan cheese. Spread this pesto over the aubergines and place under a hot grill until golden and bubbling.

Ingredients

2 aubergines
salt and pepper
4 fl oz (110ml) olive oil
1 large bunch of basil leaves
3 garlic cloves, halved
3 tbsp pine kernels, lightly toasted
3 tbsp grated Parmesan cheese

TOMATO TART

Ingredients
(serves 2-3)

10 oz (275g) puff pastry, thawed if frozen

5 oz (150g) cream cheese, (eg Boursin garlic and herb **or** onion and chive **or** fresh goat's cheese **or** plain cream cheese with a light or full fat content).

3-4 tsp pesto sauce (optional)

2 tbsp olive oil

1 lb (450g) cherry tomatoes

1 level tsp caster sugar

2-3 tbsp freshly grated Parmesan cheese

Method

On a lightly floured surface, roll out the pastry to an oblong shape about 10" x 12" (25 x 30cm) or a size and shape to fit your baking tray. Trim the edges of the pastry with a sharp knife and then slide the pastry onto the lined baking tray.

With forefinger dipped in water, dampen the edges of the pastry all round and then fold in the edges to make a 1" (2.5cm) border on all sides. With thumb and forefinger pinch the corners together where the edges meet. Chill the prepared pastry in the fridge for about 30 minutes.

Heat the oven to 425°F/220°C/gas mark 7. With a fork mash the cheese until it is soft and smooth and then spread this over the pastry case leaving the borders clear. If using the pesto sauce simply dot all over the top of the cheese.

Heat the oil in a frying pan and add the cherry tomatoes and sprinkle with the caster sugar. Stir and shake over a moderate heat for 2-3 minutes, until the tomatoes are shiny and their skins begin to split. Then spoon the tomatoes from the pan and place them all over the cheese in the tart.

Cook in the oven for 20 minutes. Halfway through the cooking time sprinkle over the grated Parmesan cheese and return to the oven for the remaining 10 minutes to complete cooking.

Garnish with chopped parsley and a few thyme leaves if liked. Serve hot, cut into thick slices.

COOL CUCUMBER CREAM SOUP

Method

Warm the oil in a pan and gently fry the spring onion with the garlic and cumin for 7-8 minutes.

Scrape this mixture into the food processor or blender jar. Add a quarter of the cucumber to start with, and when the first pieces of cucumber have liquidised, add more until completely blended.

Pour the mixture into a glass or china bowl. Stir in the yoghurt, parsley, salt and pepper, lemon juice and cayenne. Chill the soup very thoroughly and adjust the seasoning to taste when the soup is very cold.

Serve with dollops of crème fraîche or sour cream, topped with finely snipped chives, or some finely chopped walnut pieces, or even simply a little grated cucumber.

If a lighter soup is required, then chilled milk or even iced water may be stirred in to achieve the desired consistency.

Ingredients

2 tbsp olive oil
1 bunch spring onions, chopped
1 clove garlic, crushed
½ tsp cumin
2 cucumbers, peeled, deseeded and chopped (to make approx 1 lb/450g cucumber flesh)
5 fl oz (150ml) natural yoghurt
1 tbsp chopped parsley
1 tbsp chopped mint leaves
salt and pepper
juice of ½ lemon
pinch of cayenne pepper
5 fl oz (150ml) créme fraîche **or** sour cream

SAVOURY COURGETTE SOUFFLE

Method

Blend or process the courgettes, sour cream, onion, salt, eggs, cream cheese and Cheddar cheese until smooth.

Pour the mixture into 4 (6 if a smaller size) greased and lined ramekins.

Bake in the oven at 375°F/190°C/gas mark 5 for 30 minutes. Turn out and serve.

Ingredients

6 oz (175g) courgettes, grated
4 fl oz (110ml) sour cream
3 oz (75g) onion, grated
½ tsp salt
4 eggs
4 oz (110g) cream cheese, softened
3 oz (75g) Cheddar cheese, grated

A VEGETABLE SOUP
with Basil Dressing

Ingredients

6oz (175g) dried haricot beans, soaked overnight and cooked until tender **or** 15oz (425g) can cannellini beans, drained

4 tbsp water

2 carrots, diced

2 leeks, sliced into discs

1lb (450g) courgettes, cut into large cubes **or** 1lb (450g) peeled marrow or pumpkin

2 sticks celery, finely sliced

6 oz (175g) turnip, diced

2 medium potatoes, diced

3½ pints (2 litres) cold water

1 stock cube, crumbled

bouquet garni

2 oz (50g) small pasta shells**or** noodles, cooked until just tender

4 oz (110g) frozen petit pois

Method

In a large pot, over a gentle heat, place 4 tablespoons of olive oil and 4 tablespoons of water followed by the carrots, leeks, courgettes, celery and turnip. Cook for about 10-12 minutes, stirring frequently. Do not allow the vegetables to brown.

Add the diced potato and then pour the cold water over the vegetables with the crumbled stock cube and bouquet garni. Bring to the boil, then simmer for about 35 minutes.

Add the pasta and peas and continue to simmer until everything is cooked – another 10-15 minutes, adding the cooked beans to heat through for the last 5 minutes, and at the same time removing the bouquet garni.

The soup should be fairly thick but while cooking add more boiling water if necessary and during the cooking time, if not already prepared, you can make the pesto-style paste (see recipe on facing page).

To Serve: Remove the soup from the heat and season to taste with salt and pepper. Add the basil paste and stir it through. Serve with extra grated Parmesan on the side. Finely chopped parsley makes a good garnish.

BASIL DRESSING
(Traditional method when fresh basil is available)

Method

Pound the peeled garlic with the basil and tomatoes in a mortar and then stir in the Parmesan and oil to form a paste (yes, you can use a blender if you wish).

Ingredients

3 cloves garlic

10 basil leaves

2 oz (50g) Parmesan cheese, grated

2 large tomatoes, peeled, deseeded and mashed with a fork

4 tbsp of olive oil

• The alternative dressing recipe is to add at least 4 heaped dessertspoons of a bottled pesto sauce to 1 fat crushed garlic clove and a mashed tomato plus 2 tablespoons of olive oil.

• Do not add the basil 'dressing' until just before serving the soup. If you wish to make the soup and reheat for use later in the day, or if you don't want to use it all in one go, then serve the soup in individual bowls and then stir in the basil to taste. Remember to save some!

GAZPACHO

Ingredients

2 tbsp fresh breadcrumbs
3 tbsp olive oil
3 tbsp red wine vinegar
1¼ lb (560g) tomatoes, skinned
10 oz (275g) cucumber, skinned and finely chopped
1 green pepper, deseeded and chopped
1 red pepper, deseeded and chopped
1-3 crushed cloves garlic
¾ pint (450ml) water
salt and pepper
2 tbsp mixed fresh chopped herbs eg parsley, chives and marjoram (optional but highly recommended)
3 slices fresh white bread, crusts removed
oil for frying

Method

Place the breadcrumbs, olive oil and vinegar in a mixing bowl. Leave to soak for 20 minutes.

Halve the tomatoes and chop the flesh. Keep aside in the refrigerator about 2 tablespoons of each chopped vegetable.

Puree the remaining vegetables, with the garlic and half the water until quite smooth. Gradually add this to the oil and breadcrumb mixture, stirring in well.

Then add the remaining water, season with salt and pepper to taste and stir in the herbs. Cover and chill in the refrigerator for 2 hours before serving.

Meanwhile cut the bread into cubes. Heat the oil, add the bread and fry until golden brown. Drain well on absorbent kitchen paper.

Serve the soup well chilled accompanied with the reserved chopped vegetables and croutons in side dishes. Add one or two ice cubes to each bowl of soup before serving, if wished.

TOMATOES PROVENÇAL

Method

Preheat the oven to 400°F/200°C/gas mark 6. Place the tomatoes, cut side up , in a shallow baking dish.

Sprinkle the salt, pepper, garlic, parsley and breadcrumbs evenly over the tomatoes. Drizzle the olive oil over the top.

Bake in the oven for 10-15 minutes, or until the tomatoes are tender but not falling apart.

Any left-over is very good chopped up and spread on toast.

Ingredients

8 large tomatoes, halved
salt and pepper
3 cloves garlic, finely chopped
2 tbsp finely chopped parsley
2 tbsp fresh breadcrumbs
2 tbsp olive oil

MATCHSTICK CUCUMBER AND PEAS

Method

Rinse the cucumber and cut into matchsticks. Cut a piece of foil large enough to seal the vegetables.

In a large bowl mix all the ingredients together lightly and then pile onto the foil. Season well with salt and pepper. Seal them in completely and steam over boiling water for 8 minutes.

Remove the foil and garnish the vegetables with sprigs of mint. Serve at once.

Ingredients

1 cucumber
4 oz (110g) fresh peas,
  podded (or frozen)
1 tsp lemon juice
1 tsp chopped mint
1 tsp sugar
1 oz (25g) butter
salt and pepper
sprigs of mint to garnish

COURGETTE SALAD

Ingredients
1lb (450g) courgettes
4 tbsp olive oil
2 shallots, finely chopped
1½ tsp paprika
salt and pepper
1½ tsp brown sugar
1 tsp dill
3 tbsp white wine vinegar

Method
Trim the ends of the unpeeled courgettes and slice them fairly thinly into discs or sticks.

Heat the oil and add the shallots and courgettes and cook over a low heat, stirring occasionally, for about 5 minutes. Do not brown the vegetables, just allow them to soften.

Then add the remaining ingredients and cook for another 2-3 minutes.

Place in a serving dish and garnish with finely chopped parsley. Can be eaten hot, warm or cool, but not chilled.

COURGETTES IN SWEET AND SOUR SAUCE

Ingredients
1½ lb (700g) courgettes
1 tbsp olive oil
1 large onion, finely chopped
1 tbsp malt vinegar
1 tbsp soy sauce
1 tbsp sultanas
1 tbsp almonds
¼ tsp powdered cloves
2 tbsp honey
1 tbsp grated dark chocolate
  (optional)
salt and pepper
finely chopped parsley to
  garnish

Method
Cut the unpeeled courgettes into ½" (1cm) slices or 1" (2.5cm) sticks. Heat the oil in a large saucepan and cook the onion until soft.

Add the courgettes, stir well and then add the rest of the ingredients. Stir and cook for another 10-15 minutes.

BROCCOLI GRATIN

Method

Butter a shallow baking tin or gratin dish and arrange broccoli in one layer. Sprinkle with half the melted butter.

Mix together the breadcrumbs, cheese and walnuts with a touch of salt and pepper and sprinkle this mixture all over the broccoli. Sprinkle over remaining melted butter and bake in a hot oven for about 8 minutes.

For an extra brown topping you can pop it under the grill if wished. Serve hot.

Ingredients
(serves 4-6)

1½ lbs (700g) broccoli florets, boiled until just tender then rinsed with cold water and drained
2 oz (50g) butter, melted
salt and pepper
2 oz (50g) Gruyère cheese, grated
1 oz (25g) chopped walnuts
2 oz (50g) fresh white breadcrumbs

CREAMED CARROTS

Method

Boil the carrots until tender, in lightly salted water, then drain and mash well.

Melt the butter in a saucepan. Add the mashed carrots, salt, pepper and nutmeg. Stir in the cream and cook gently, stirring until absorbed.

Serve hot. Will keep, covered, for 2 days in the fridge.

Ingredients
(serves 4-6)

2 lbs (1kg) carrots peeled and cut into chunks
salt
1 oz (30g) butter
4 tbsp double cream
pepper
pinch of nutmeg
pinch of sugar

CREAM OF PARSNIP SOUP

Ingredients
(serves 6)

2 oz (50g) unsalted butter
1 large onion, chopped
1 leek, white part only, washed and chopped
1 small green chilli pepper, deseeded and chopped **or** 1 tsp chilli flakes
½ tsp sugar
½ tsp grated fresh ginger root
½ tsp ground turmeric
pinch freshly grated nutmeg
1 lb (450g) parsnips (peeled weight), chopped
1 large potato, peeled and chopped
1½ pints (850ml) chicken **or** vegetable stock
1¼ pints (720ml) water
salt and pepper
lemon juice
6 tbsp cream
crisp bacon bits (optional)

Method

Melt the butter in a large saucepan over a medium heat. Add the onion, leek, chilli pepper, sugar, ginger root, turmeric and nutmeg. Cook, stirring, for 5 minutes.

Add the parsnips and potato and continue to cook, stirring occasionally for 5 minutes. Add the stock and water to the vegetable mixture, bring to the boil and then reduce the heat and simmer, uncovered, until the vegetables are tender, for about 20 minutes.

Add salt and pepper to taste and allow to cool. Puree the soup in batches in a food processor or blender.

To serve the soup hot, reheat gently without boiling and serve with a tablespoon of cream in each bowl, a squeeze of lemon juice and chopped parsley. The crisp bacon bits are an optional extra.

PARSNIP PATTIES

Peel, boil and then mash 1 lb (450g) of parsnips with seasoning to taste. Shape into patties (makes 4 large ones) and coat with fine dried breadcrumbs all over.

Gently fry in hot oil in a shallow pan, turning once to brown on both sides. Excellent served with grills or roasts or on their own with apple sauce.

PARSNIPS GLAZED WITH CIDER

Method

Preheat the oven to 400°F/200°C/gas mark 6. Peel the parsnips and cut into quarters lengthways. Cook in boiling salted water until just tender and then drain.

Put the parsnips into a shallow ovenproof dish. Sprinkle with the sugar and pour over the cider. Dot with butter and season with salt and pepper.

Bake in the oven for 20 minutes, basting occasionally during cooking.

Ingredients

12-18 small parsnips
3 tbsp brown sugar
6-8 tbsp cider
3 oz (75g) butter
salt and pepper

PARSNIP CRISPS

Simply peel some parsnips and then remove strips from the length of the vegetable and deep fry in hot oil until golden brown.

COLLEGE CAULIFLOWER

Ingredients
1 cauliflower
4 oz (110g) pasta shells
4 oz (110g) ham
4 tomatoes, skinned, deseeded and quartered
2 oz (50g) butter
2 leeks, finely sliced
1" (2.5cm) piece fresh ginger peeled and grated
1 clove garlic, crushed
2 tbsp flour
¼ pint (150ml) chicken stock
¼ pint (150ml) milk
¼ pint (150ml) dry white wine **or** cider
4 oz (110g) Cheddar cheese, grated
salt and pepper
3 tbsp double cream
5 ginger nut biscuits
1 heaped tsp Dijon mustard
chopped parsley to garnish

Method
Divide the cauliflower into florets and chop the stalk into dice. Cook the cauliflower in boiling salted water until just tender, drain and place in an ovenproof serving dish.

Cook the pasta until just tender, drain and combine with the cauliflower. Add the ham, cut into strips. Arrange the tomato pieces on top of the cauliflower.

Heat the butter in a pan, add the leeks, ginger and garlic and cook over a very low heat, stirring to prevent sticking, for about 8 minutes or until the leeks are soft. Add the flour and mix well.

Gradually blend in the stock, milk and wine (see note below), whisking continually over a medium heat until the sauce comes to the boil and is thick and smooth. Add half the cheese and continue to cook over a medium heat for 3 minutes, stirring all the time. Season with salt and pepper, reduce the heat and mix in the cream. Pour the sauce over the cauliflower mixture.

Crush the biscuits into fairly fine crumbs, mix them with the mustard and remaining cheese. Sprinkle the mixture over the top of the dish and bake in the oven at 350°F/180°C/gas mark 4 for 20 minutes. Finish under a hot grill if necessary for a few minutes until the top is bubbling, crisp and golden brown.

Serve at once with a good sprinkling of finely chopped parsley.

• If the stock, milk and wine are combined before adding to the leeks a slight curdling effect may occur, however diligent whisking of the sauce will ensure a smooth result.

BULGAR WHEAT SALAD
(TABBOULEH)

Method

Place the bulgar in a bowl, adding 8 fl oz (225ml) boiling water. Leave to soak for 30 minutes. Then drain well, pressing out the excess water.

Wash the lettuce, cut away the core and separate into leaves. Line a salad bowl with some of the lettuce and shred the rest. Combine with all the remaining ingredients and then spoon into the salad bowl.

Garnish with lemon wedges before serving.

Ingredients

4 oz (110g) bulgar (cracked
  processed wheat)
1 lettuce
2-3 tbsp finely chopped
  parsley
4 shallots **or** spring onions,
  finely chopped
1 tbsp finely chopped mint
4 oz (110g) diced cucumber
  (optional)
juice of 1 lemon
salt and pepper to taste
3 ripe tomatoes, peeled,
  deseeded and finely chopped
  or 8-10 cherry tomatoes,
  halved
2 fl oz (50ml) olive oil
lemon wedges

CAKES & DESSERTS

BUTTERED BRAMLEY APPLE CREAM

Ingredients
(serves 5-6)

1 lb (450g) cooking apples
grated rind and juice of 1 large orange
3 tbsp medium to sweet white wine
2-4 oz (50-110g) sugar
1 tbsp orange flower water
4 oz (110g) unsalted butter, softened
½ pint (300ml) double cream, whipped to soft peaks

Method

Peel and core the apples and then cut into chunks. Put the apples into a pan with the orange rind and juice and the white wine. Cook the apples over a low heat until they are softened and pulped.

Stir in the sugar, to taste, and flower water. Then blend the mixture to a fine puree, allowing the fruit to cool down to just warm. Blend in the softened butter and then fold in the cream.

Spoon into a bowl or glasses and chill well before serving.

JAFFA LOAF

Method

Sift the dry ingredients into a bowl. Add the oil, orange juice and rind and using an electric beater mix for 1 minute. Add the eggs and vanilla and beat for 45 seconds until well mixed together. Pour into an oiled and lined 2lb (900g) loaf tin.

Bake in the oven at 325°F/170°C/gas mark 3 in the centre of the oven for 1 hour. Leave in the tin for 5 minutes before turning out onto a wire rack to cool completely.

Then heat the butter and juice for the glaze in a small pan, add the icing sugar and stir over a very low heat until smooth. Pour over the top of the cold cake and decorate with a little finely grated orange zest.

Ingredients

9 oz (250g) plain flour
6 oz (175g) caster sugar
2 tsp baking powder
generous pinch of salt
4 fl oz (110ml) oil
4 fl oz (110ml) fresh orange juice
1 tsp finely grated orange rind
2 eggs
few drops vanilla essence
for the orange glaze:
2 tbsp orange juice
½ oz (15g) butter
6 oz (175g) icing sugar, sifted

BRAN LOAF

Method

Place the sugar, All Bran, dried fruit, orange zest, golden syrup and milk in a bowl and stir well together. Leave to soak overnight.

Next day, add the beaten egg, mashed banana and flour and mix well. Turn into a greased 2 lb (1kg) loaf tin and bake in the oven at 350°F/180°C/gas mark 4 for about 1hr 30 mins, until cooked, or until a skewer inserted in the centre comes out clean.

Turn out onto a wire rack to cool slightly. Delicious served still warm with butter.

Ingredients

8 oz (225g) soft brown sugar
4 oz (110g) All Bran
8 oz (225g) mixed dried fruit
grated zest of 1 orange
1 tbsp golden syrup
8 fl oz (250ml) milk
1 egg, beaten
1 large banana, peeled and mashed
4 oz (110g) self-raising flour

RUM PRUNE PUDDING
with Greek Lemon Cream

Ingredients
8 oz (225g) ready to eat
prunes, halved
3-4 tbsp rum (see note)
12-16 slices of French bread
about ½" (1cm) thick
1 tsp butter
6 eggs
3 oz (75g) caster sugar
2 oz (50g) soft light brown
sugar
8 fl oz (225ml) whipping
cream
1 pint (600ml) milk
2 tsp grated orange zest
icing sugar

Method
Combine the prunes and rum in a bowl and leave for at least 1-2 hours. Butter a baking dish and line the bottom with half of the bread slices. Spoon the prunes over the bread, then cover with the remaining bread overlapping the slices slightly.

Whisk together the eggs, sugars and cream, then stir in the orange zest and milk. Pour over the bread, pressing down lightly to saturate completely. Bake in the lower half of the oven at 400°F/200°C/gas mark 6 for 40-50 minutes until just set (cover with foil if necessary to prevent overbrowning).

Allow to cool for 15 minutes before serving, dusting the top with icing sugar. Serve with cream, ice cream or this delicious Greek Lemon Cream.

• Instead of rum or any other desired spirit, a non-alcoholic version can be made using 3 tablespoons of hot tea with 1 teaspoon of vanilla essence.

GREEK LEMON CREAM

Ingredients
¾ pint (450g) Greek natural
yoghurt
¼ pint (150g) double cream
4 oz (110g) caster sugar
juice of 2 lemons
grated zest of ½ lemon

Method
Place the sugar in a bowl. Add lemon juice and zest followed by the yoghurt and cream and mix together well.

Serve chilled or freeze in a plastic container for 3 hours, then mix well with a fork and return to freezer until needed. Allow to soften a little before serving.

• Experience has shown that it's wise to make double the amount given above!

BAKEWELL PUDDING

Method

Roll out the pastry thinly and line the 9" (23cm) tin. Spread the jam all over the bottom of the pastry (gentle warming in a saucepan will make this very much easier).

Gently melt the butter and place the sugar and lemon rind in a bowl. Beat the melted butter into the sugar and lemon rind until the mixture is smooth and glossy. Then add the beaten eggs, beating in a little at a time.

In another bowl mix the cake crumbs and ground almonds together and then fold them into the egg mixture (do this in batches with a metal spoon). Add the lemon juice to give a dropping consistency. Put the mixture into the pastry case and smooth level with a knife.

Bake in a hot oven 425°F/220°C/gas mark 7 for about 15 minutes to start browning, then reduce the heat to 350°F/180°C/gas mark 4 for a further 20-30 minutes until the filling feels lightly firm to the touch.

Serve hot or cold with cream or custard.

Ingredients

for a 9" (23cm) flan tin:

6 oz (175g) puff pastry, thawed if frozen

2-3 tbsp strawberry jam

3 oz (75g) butter **or** margarine

3 oz (75g) caster sugar

grated rind and juice of ½ lemon

2 eggs, beaten

4 oz (110g) Madeira cake crumbs

4 oz (110g) ground almonds

If using a 7" (18cm) pie plate then reduce the ingredients as follows:

4 oz (110g) pastry, 2 tbsp jam, 2 oz (50g) butter, 2 oz (50g) caster sugar, 1 egg, 3 oz (75g) cake crumbs, 3 oz (75g) ground almonds.

MARMALADE SPICE CAKE

Ingredients

6 oz (175g) butter **or**
   margarine, softened
8 tbsp golden syrup
2 large eggs, beaten
10 level tbsp medium cut
   orange marmalade
12 oz (350g) self-raising flour
1 level tsp baking powder
1 level tsp ground nutmeg
1 level tsp ground cinnamon
¼ tsp ground cloves
approx ¼ pint (150ml) milk
2 oz (50g) cornflakes
oil

Method

Grease and base line an 8" (20 cm) square or 9" (23 cm) round cake tin.

In a large bowl beat together the softened butter with 6 tablespoons of the golden syrup until well mixed together. Then beat in the eggs, and when well mixed stir in 5 tablespoons of the marmalade.

Mix in the sifted flour and baking powder, along with the nutmeg, cinnamon and cloves, adding a little milk, if needed, to give the mixture a fairly stiff consistency. Turn into the prepared tin and level the surface.

Crush the cornflakes and in a bowl mix together with the remaining syrup and marmalade. Carefully spread this over the top of the cake mixture.

Bake in the oven at 350°F/180°C/gas mark 4 for about 1 hour 10 minutes. Turn out to cool on a wire rack.

• This cake will freeze well. To use, thaw at room temperature for 6 hours.

FARMHOUSE FRUIT LOAF

Method

Sift the flour into a large bowl and add the butter, cut into small dice. Rub the butter into the flour, using your fingers, until the mixture resembles fine breadcrumbs. Add the raisins, dates or figs, apple, walnuts and sugar and mix everything together well.

In another bowl mix together the baking powder, bicarbonate of soda, milk and honey or syrup and stir this mixture into the dry ingredients. The final mixture should have a stiff dropping consistency. If needed you can add a little more milk.

Spoon the mixture into a greased and lined 2 lb (900g) loaf tin and bake in the centre of the oven at 350°F/180°C/gas mark 4 for 1¼-1½ hours, or until the loaf is well risen and firm to the touch. Turn out onto a wire rack to cool.

Ingredients
(for I loaf)

8 oz (225g) plain flour
4 oz (110g) butter
4 oz (110g) seedless raisins
1 oz (110g) dates **or** figs, chopped
4 oz (110g) apple, peeled, cored and chopped
2 oz (50g) chopped walnuts
2 oz (50g) soft brown sugar
I tsp baking powder
I tsp bicarbonate of soda
¼ pint (150ml) milk
3 tbsp runny honey **or** syrup

APRICOT CAKE

Ingredients

4 oz (110g) glace cherries
4 oz (110g) dried apricots, chopped
1 lb (450g) mixed fruit
5 oz (150g) butter **or** margarine
6 fl oz (175ml) red wine
6 oz (175g) golden syrup
2 oz (50g) chopped nuts (optional)
8 oz (225g) granary flour
1 tsp mixed spice
½ tsp bicarbonate of soda
2 eggs, beaten

Method

Preheat the oven to 300°F/150°C/gas mark 2. Grease and line an 8" (20cm) cake tin.

Place all the fruit, butter and wine in a saucepan and bring slowly to the boil. Simmer gently for 5 minutes and then remove from the heat and allow to cool.

When cooled, stir in the remaining ingredients, beat everything together well and then pour the mixture into the prepared tin.

Bake in the oven for 1¾-2 hours (see note). Cool in the tin for 1 hour and then cool completely on a wire rack. Will keep wrapped in foil for 1 week.

• The baking time is approximate, depending on the individual oven used but the usual skewer or cake tester method will indicate when it is done.

ETON MESS

Ingredients

(serves 4-6)
500g (1 lb) strawberries
55ml (2 fl oz) orange liqueur, whisky or kirsch
finely grated zest of one orange
450ml (15 fl oz) double or whipping cream
6 meringue shells broken into small pieces

Method

Hull and slice the strawberries into a bowl, sprinkle over the liqueur and orange zest, mix lightly and if time allows chill for 1 hour.

Whip the cream to the soft peak stage and fold into the strawberries with the meringue.

Serve in tall glasses with a teaspoon. Mint leaves and a crisp sweet biscuit would make an ideal garnish.

TWO TERRIFIC TARTS

RASPBERRY TART

Method

Preheat the oven to 375°F/190°C/gas mark 5. Place the egg yolks in a large bowl and beat with a fork. Pour in the cream and the granulated sugar and mix together until thoroughly blended.

Pour the mixture into the cooked and cooled pastry shell. Arrange the raspberries in a single layer all over the top of the cream. Cook in the centre of the oven until the cream filling begins to set, about 20-30 minutes.

Sprinkle with caster sugar and leave to cool completely before serving.

Ingredients

3 large egg yolks
6 fl oz (175ml) double cream
2 oz (50g) granulated sugar
9-10" (23-25.5 cm) pre-baked shortcrust pastry shell
8-10 oz (225-275g) fresh raspberries
2 tsp icing sugar

FRUIT AND ALMOND TART

Method

Preheat the oven to 375°F/190°C/gas mark 5. In a large bowl thoroughly blend together the almonds, egg, granulated sugar, kirsch and crème fraîche, until quite smooth.

Arrange the prepared fruit in the cooked, cooled pastry shell. Carefully pour the cream filling all over the top. Cook in the centre of the oven until the cream filling has set, about 45 minutes.

Remove from the oven and sprinkle with caster sugar. Serve warm or at room temperature with cream or ice cream.

Ingredients

5 oz (150g) ground almonds
1 large egg, lightly beaten
2-3 oz (50-75g) granulated sugar
2 tbsp kirsch liqueur
6 fl oz (175ml) crème fraîche **or** double cream
1-1¼ lb (450-570g) sliced or diced fruit (pears, peaches, cherries, plums or nectarines)
9-10" (23-25.5cm) pre-baked shortcrust pastry shell
1 tbsp caster sugar

STRAWBERRY FLAN

Ingredients

(serves 6)
for the pastry:
3½ oz (100g) butter, softened
3 tbsp icing sugar
1 egg yolk
few drops vanilla essence
5 oz (150g) plain flour
pinch of salt

for the filling:
1¼ lb (570g) strawberries
9 oz (250g) cream cheese
6½ fl oz (200ml) double
  cream
3 tbsp icing sugar
1 tsp finely grated orange rind
1 tbsp Grand Marnier **or** few
  drops of vanilla essence
2 tbsp seedless strawberry or
  raspberry jam
1 tsp water
whipped cream or pouring
  cream to serve

Method

In a large bowl, cream the butter and icing sugar and beat in the egg yolk and vanilla. Sift the flour with salt and add to the bowl. Form into a soft dough ball, place in a polythene bag and chill in the fridge for about 1 hour.

Press thinly into the base of a 9" (23cm) loose-bottomed flan ring. Prick the base and sides of the pastry and bake in the oven at 400°F/200°C/gas mark 6 for 10-12 minutes until pale biscuit in colour. When cold, remove the ring and put the flan case onto a serving plate.

In a bowl whisk the cream cheese, double cream, icing sugar, orange rind and liqueur or vanilla until thick. Spoon evenly into pastry shell and arrange the strawberries on top of the filling to cover completely.

To glaze the flan, heat the jam and water together and then brush over the berries. Chill lightly and serve.

WHITE CELEBRATION CAKE

Method

Preheat the oven to 325°F/170°C/gas mark 3. Cream the butter and sugar together in a large bowl. Then beat in the eggs and fold in the sieved flours. Stir in all the mixed fruit and nuts with the pineapple or lemon juice.

Turn the mixture into a greased and lined 8" (20cm) cake tin. Smooth the top level, then make a slight hollow in the centre. Tie a double layer of brown paper around the tin wide enough to stand 3" (7.5cm) above the top of the tin.

Bake in the oven for 2-2½ hours or until a thin wooden skewer comes out clean from the centre of the cake. Cool in the tin for 30 minutes, then turn out onto a wire rack.

Ingredients

- 8 oz (225g) butter
- 5 oz (150g) caster sugar
- 4 large eggs
- 4 oz (110g) plain flour
- 4 oz (110g) self-raising flour
- 2 oz (50g) cornflour
- 6 oz (175g) glace cherries, halved
- 4 oz (110g) glace pineapple, roughly chopped
- 2 oz (50g) crystallised ginger, chopped
- 4 oz (110g) mixed glace fruits, roughly chopped
- 2 oz (50g) candied peel, chopped
- 1½ oz (40g) angelica, diced
- 2 oz (50g) blanched almonds, roughly chopped
- 2 oz (50g) blanched hazelnuts, roughly chopped
- 1 tbsp pineapple **or** lemon juice

PINEAPPLE CAKE

Ingredients

4 oz (110g) butter
6 oz (175g) soft brown sugar
7 oz (200g) canned crushed pineapple, drained (see note)
12 oz (350g) mixed dried fruit
4 oz (110g) glace cherries, halved
8 oz (225g) self-raising flour
1 tsp mixed spice
2 eggs, beaten

Method

Put the butter, sugar, pineapple, mixed dried fruit and glace cherries into a saucepan. Heat gently together and allow to melt. Then increase the heat until the mixture comes to the boil. Take off the heat and leave to cool.

When cool, stir in the sifted flour and mixed spice. Mix in the beaten eggs and blend everything well together. Pour into a greased and lined 7" (18cm) cake tin or a 2lb (900g) loaf tin and bake in the oven at 300°F/150°C/gas mark 2 for about 1 hour 40 minutes.

• In the unlikely event of finding crushed pineapple unavailable, simply whizz up in a blender a similar weight of pineapple chunks or rings.

STRAWBERRY SYLLABUB

Ingredients

(serves 4-6)
1 small glass sweet white wine
2 tbsp kirsch
grated zest of ½ lemon
juice of 1 lemon
2 oz (50g) caster sugar
½ pint (300ml) double cream
grated nutmeg, to taste
10-12 oz (275-350g) strawberries

Method

In a glass bowl, mix together the wine, kirsch, lemon zest and juice and then add the sugar and stir until it dissolves.

Pour in the cream plus a little nutmeg and whisk until lightly thickened. Slice 4 oz (110g) of the strawberries into quarters and fold into the cream.

Blend the remaining strawberries in a blender (or mash thoroughly) and spoon equal amounts into 4-6 glasses. Pour syllabub on the top and serve chilled.

Garnish with mint sprigs and thin sweet biscuits.

PUFF PASTRY PUDDING

Method

Preheat the oven to 375°F/190°C/gas mark 5. Grease a round, glass or ceramic ovenproof dish and add the crumbled pastry. Add the nuts and lemon juice and mix through.

Heat the milk, sugar and cinnamon to just below boiling point, then slowly add the beaten eggs. Pour this mixture over the pastry in the dish and then sprinkle with rosewater.

Pour the cream all over the top and then bake in the oven for about 30 minutes, until golden. Serve at once.

Pouring cream or soft vanilla ice-cream are the ideal companions to this pudding, plus a little seasonal fruit salad on the side if wished, for contrast and colour.

Ingredients

10 oz (275g) cooked puff pastry, crumbled (see note)
2½ oz (60g) fresh shelled pistachio nuts, chopped
2½ oz (60g) flaked almonds, browned in the oven
1 tbsp lemon juice
12 fl oz (330ml) milk
6 oz (175g) sugar
pinch of cinnamon
2 eggs, beaten
2 tsp rosewater
½ pint (300ml) double cream

• To prepare the puff pastry, roll out the dough and cut into strips. Bake in a hot oven until well browned and crisp.

Allow the pastry to cool a little, then break it up with your fingers into a large mixing bowl, or directly into the buttered baking dish if you intend to proceed with the recipe immediately.

The pastry can be made well in advance and kept in an airtight container.

CHRISTMAS CAKE

Ingredients

1 lb 6 oz (625g) sultanas
6 oz (175g) pitted prunes, chopped
6 oz (175g) raisins
9 oz (250g) glace cherries, quartered
5 oz (150g) mixed peel, chopped
11 oz (310g) plain flour
1 tsp ground cinnamon
2 tsp ground mixed spice
½ tsp grated nutmeg
8 oz (225g) unsalted butter
8 oz (225g) soft, light brown sugar
5 eggs, size 3, beaten
1½ tbsp black treacle
5 tbsp brandy
5 oz (150g) walnuts, chopped
9" (23cm) round cake tin, greased and lined

Method

Preheat the oven to 300°F/150°C/gas mark 2. In a large bowl thoroughly mix together all the fruits. Sift the flour into another bowl with the spices.

In a third bowl cream together the butter and sugar until pale and light. Gradually add the eggs and the treacle. With a metal spoon fold in the flour, then mix in the brandy, walnuts and fruit.

Spoon the mixture into the tin, smooth the surface, then make a slight hollow in the centre. Line the outside of the cake tin with a sheet of brown paper which should come 2-3"(5-7.5cm) above the rim of the tin.

Cook in the oven for 3½-4 hours. Cover with greaseproof paper after 1½ hours to avoid over-browning. The cake is cooked when a skewer inserted into the centre comes out clean.

Leave to cool in the tin. Remove the lining paper and wrap in fresh greaseproof paper and foil. Store in a cool dry place for up to 2 months.

ROYAL APPLE PUDDING

Method

Remove the cores from the apples and then peel them. Sprinkle the whole apples with lemon juice and sugar and keep to one side.

In a bowl cream together the butter and sugar. Beat in the egg yolks, juice of half a lemon and the grated lemon rind. Sift the flour and baking powder into the mixture and then add the milk and rum. Mix everything together thoroughly until smooth.

In another bowl whisk the egg whites until stiff and fold them carefully into the mixture, using a metal spoon. Pour the mixture into a buttered 9" (23cm) cake tin or oven-proof dish.

Press the apples into the mixture and then brush the cake with melted butter and beaten egg yolk. Bake in the oven at 325°F/170°C/gas mark 3 for approximately 1 hour, until risen and golden brown.

Remove from the oven and sprinkle with icing sugar.

Ingredients

6 medium-sized eating apples
juice of ½ lemon
2 oz (50g) caster sugar
for the batter:
2 oz (50g) butter
4 oz (110g) caster sugar
2 egg yolks
juice of ½ lemon
grated rind of ½ lemon
4 oz (110g) self-raising flour
1 tsp baking powder
3 fl oz (75ml) milk
3 tbsp rum
3 egg whites
1 oz (25g) butter, for greasing
for the glaze:
1 oz (25g) butter, melted
1 egg yolk
3 tbsp icing sugar to dust

APPLE CREAM CUSTARD TART

Ingredients

12 oz (350g) shortcrust
pastry, blind baked
2 large Bramley apples (about
1½lb/700g unpeeled weight)
5 oz (150g) caster sugar
½ tsp powdered cinnamon
2 tbsp Calvados **or** brandy
3 egg yolks
7 fl oz (200ml) double cream
2 oz (50g) flaked almonds

Method

First roll out the pastry and use to line a 9 or 10"
(23-25.5 cm) flan tin and bake blind at 400°F/
200°C/gas mark 6 for 15 minutes (see note).

Then peel, core, quarter and cut the apples into
bite-sized pieces. Sprinkle 2 tablespoons of the
sugar on the pastry case followed by the cinnamon.
Spread the apple pieces on top of the sugar.

Lightly whisk together the egg yolks, remaining
sugar and brandy in a bowl, then pour in the
cream, still whisking. Pour this mixture carefully
over the apples and bake in the oven at 350°F/
180°C/gas mark 4 for 45 minutes. Scatter the
flaked almonds on top and bake for a further 15
minutes.

Serve the tart warm or cold with cream or
softened vanilla ice cream.

• If uncertain about the strength of your pastry the flan can be baked in the tin,
preferably one with a loose bottom for ease of removal. In any event do allow the
pastry to cool down and set before attempting to cut or remove to a serving plate.

• Depending on the depth of your flan case there may be a little of the custard
mixture left over which can be cooked separately in a small ramekin. Use a baking
tray.

AKENFIELD CAKE

Method

Preheat the oven to 350°F/180°C/gas mark 4. Grease and flour a 9" (23cm) springform cake tin. A flan or sandwich tin can be used instead, provided it is 1½" (4cm) deep.

In a bowl, cream the sugars with the butter until they are soft and fluffy. Sift the flour with the baking powder, salt and spices. Gradually beat the eggs into the creamed mixture then fold in the flour.

Stir in the apples, ginger and raisins. The cake mixture should be fairly soft; if not stir in 1-2 tablespoons of milk.

Turn the cake mixture into the prepared tin, smooth level and bake in the oven for 40-50 minutes until firm to a light touch.

Leave the cake in the tin to cool a little, then turn out onto a wire rack to cool completely. To decorate dust the top of the cake with a little caster sugar.

The cake can be served now, but for an extra glamorous presentation whip the cream until softly stiff and spoon a little into the ends of each of the brandy snaps. Arrange these in a circle on top of the cake.

Pipe or spoon cream in between each brandy snap and top this with a slice of stem ginger, plus fruit if using. A fresh flower in the centre will provide the perfect touch.

Ingredients

3 oz (75g) caster sugar
3 oz (75g) soft brown sugar
4 oz (110g) butter, at room temperature **or** soft margarine
8 oz (225g) plain flour
2 level tsp baking powder
½ level tsp salt
1 level tsp ground cinnamon
1 level tsp ground ginger
2 eggs
8 oz (225g) eating apples, peeled, cored and coarsely grated
4 pieces stem ginger, finely chopped
2 oz (50g) raisins
2 tbsp milk (optional)
caster sugar to dust

for special decoration:
5 fl oz (150ml) fresh double cream
8 brandy snaps
8 thin slices stem ginger
8 fresh raspberries, if available

SUNFLOWER HONEY BREAD

Ingredients

8 oz (225g) sunflower seeds
6 oz (175g) wholemeal self-
  raising flour
1 tsp baking powder
1 tsp salt
2 eggs
2 oz (50g) butter
3 fl oz (75ml) clear honey
8 fl oz (225ml) milk

Method

Preheat the oven to 350°F/180°C/gas mark 4. Using a blender, coffee grinder or pestle and mortar, grind 4 oz (110g) of the sunflower seeds into a coarse flour. Combine this with the wholemeal flour, baking powder and salt. Mix well together.

In another bowl beat together the eggs, softened butter, honey and milk, then stir this mixture into the flour mixture. Keeping ½ oz (10g) aside for the topping, add the remaining sunflower seeds and mix well.

Transfer the mixture to a lightly oiled 2 lb (900g) loaf tin and sprinkle the reserved sunflower seeds over the top. Bake in the oven for 1 hour or until a skewer inserted into the centre comes out clean.

Remove from the oven and leave to cool in the tin. Very good spread with butter or cream cheese, with an extra trickle of honey or golden syrup.

AVOCADO CREAM SOUP

Method

Halve the avocados and remove the stones. Carefully scoop out the flesh and place in the food processor or blender.

Add the onion, lemon rind and juice, yoghurt and soured cream and then blend everything together until quite smooth.

Pour the mixture into a large bowl and gradually whisk in the stock. Season to taste with salt and pepper. Cover and chill in the fridge.

Serve soup garnished with snipped chives.

Ingredients

2 ripe avocados
1 bunch of spring onions, finely chopped
grated rind and juice of 1 lemon
5 oz (150g) natural yoghurt
5 fl oz (150ml) sour cream
1 pint (600ml) vegetable **or** chicken stock
salt and pepper
snipped fresh chives

PATRICK'S MEXICAN MAGIC

GUACAMOLE

Ingredients
6 spring onions, finely
  chopped
2 large ripe avocados, stoned
  and peeled
I tbsp lime juice
2 cloves garlic, crushed
few drops of Tabasco sauce
2 tomatoes, peeled, deseeded
  and finely chopped
1-2 tbsp sour cream (optional)
I tbsp chopped coriander

Method
Place the chopped spring onions in a bowl and add the avocado flesh. Mash together with a fork. Then add the lime juice, garlic and Tabasco and mash together until well blended. Put the blended mixture into a serving bowl.

Carefully stir in the chopped tomatoes and sour cream, if using. Season to taste with salt and pepper and then mix in half the coriander. Just before serving sprinkle with the remaining coriander.

Serve as a dip or in hollowed out tomato halves as an accompaniment.

TOMATO SALSA

Ingredients
4 large firm **or** 8 small firm
  tomatoes
I red-skinned onion
1-2 cloves garlic, crushed
2 tbsp chopped fresh
  coriander
½ red **or** green chilli,
  deseeded and finely chopped
  (optional)
finely grated zest of ½ lime
1-2 tbsp lime juice
pepper

Method
Finely chop the tomatoes and place in a bowl. Finely slice the red onions and add to the tomatoes with the garlic and coriander. Mix together lightly.

Then add the chilli followed by lime zest and juice and mix well. Transfer to a serving bowl and sprinkle with pepper to taste.

TORTILLAS

Method

Sift the flour and salt into a bowl and add the fat. Rub the fat into the flour with the fingertips until the mixture resembles fine breadcrumbs. Add just enough water to mix to a soft dough.

Turn the dough out onto a lightly floured surface and knead until smooth (2-3 minutes). Place the dough in a plastic bag and leave to rest for 15 minutes.

Then divide the dough into 10 equal pieces and keep it covered with a damp cloth to prevent it drying out. Roll out each piece of dough individually on a lightly floured surface to a circle of 7-8" (18-20cm). Place the tortillas between sheets of paper towel as you make them.

Heat a heavy-based frying pan until just beginning to smoke. Brush off any excess flour from the tortilla and place in the pan and cook for 20-30 seconds on each side until just browning. They will bubble from the heat and should be pressed down gently with a spatula during cooking. Be careful not to burn or over-brown them.

Wrap the tortillas in a clean tea towel or between sheets of kitchen paper when cooked to keep them pliable. When they are cold, wrap in clingfilm if you are not using them at once. They will keep in the fridge for several days.

Ingredients

10 oz (275g) plain white flour
1 tsp salt
2 oz (50g) white vegetable fat
5-6 fl oz (150-175ml) warm water

CHICKEN FAJITAS

Ingredients

2 red peppers
2 green peppers
2 tbsp olive oil
2 onions, chopped
2 cloves garlic, crushed
1 chilli, deseeded and finely
  chopped
2 boneless chicken breasts
3 oz (75g) small mushrooms,
  sliced
2 tsp freshly chopped
  coriander **or** flat leaved
  parsley
grated zest of 1 lime
2 tbsp lime juice
salt and pepper
4 wheat tortillas
4-6 tbsp sour cream
to garnish:
tomato salsa
lime wedges

Method

Cut the four 'cheeks' from each of the red and green peppers. Discard any seeds or membranes. Place the pepper cheeks skin-side up, under a preheated grill and then grill until well blackened.

Leave to cool and then peel off the skins under the running cold water tap. Cut the flesh into thin slices.

Heat the oil in a pan and add the onions, garlic and chilli and fry gently until the onion has softened. Cut the chicken into narrow strips and add to the pan and stir-fry for 4-5 minutes until nearly cooked through.

Then add the peppers, mushrooms, coriander, lime zest and juice and continue to cook for 2-3 minutes. Season to taste.

Heat the tortillas wrapped in foil in the oven at 350°F/180°C/gas mark 4 for a few minutes. Place on warm plates and divide the chicken mixture between them.

Top the chicken with a spoonful of sour cream and serve garnished with tomato salsa and a wedge of lime. Guacamole too if liked!

WILD MUSHROOM PASTA

Method

In a heavy pan heat 1 oz (25g) of the butter with a tablespoon of oil and add the carrot, celery, onion, garlic and leek and cook, stirring, for about 3 minutes, without browning. Add the mushrooms and cook, stirring, for about 1 minute.

Tie the parsley, bay leaf and thyme into a bundle and add this (or the dried bouquet garni) to the pan. Add the stock and boil for 15 minutes or until the liquid has been reduced to about 3 fl oz (75ml). Add the cream and again bring to the boil and then cook, over a moderate heat for about 15 minutes.

Meanwhile for stage two, heat the remaining 1 oz (25g) of butter in a pan and add the 6 oz (175g) of chosen mushrooms. Cook, stirring for about 2 minutes, or until the mushrooms give up their liquid. Add the shallots, parsley, salt and pepper and stir to blend well. Cook about 1 minute longer and then remove from the heat.

In a large pot, bring plenty of water to the boil, add salt to taste, and cook the pasta (penne) until al dente or according to packet instructions.

While the penne is cooking sprinkle the Stage One sauce with basil and parsley. Add to the sauce the mushroom mixture and then stir to blend. When ready add the cooked, well drained, penne to this sauce and toss well. Spoon equal portions of the penne with sauce into each of four hot soup plates.

Spoon equal portions of the chopped tomatoes into the centre of each portion and sprinkle with equal amounts of pine nuts, followed by chervil or parsley.

Ingredients

stage one:
2 oz (50g) butter
1 tbsp oil
2 oz (50g) carrots, finely chopped
2 oz (50g) celery, finely chopped
4 oz (110g) onion, finely chopped
1 clove garlic, crushed
1 leek, trimmed and finely sliced
5 oz (150g) fresh mushrooms, quartered
3 fresh parsley sprigs with 1 bay leaf and 3 fresh thyme sprigs **or** 1 sachet bouquet garni
16 fl oz (450ml) vegetable **or** chicken stock
½ pint (300ml) double cream

stage two:
6 oz (175g) assorted wild **or** cultivated mushrooms, trimmed and chopped
1 oz (25g) finely chopped shallots
1 tbsp finely chopped parsley
salt and pepper to taste
16 oz (450g) penne
2 tbsp fresh torn basil leaves
2 tbsp fresh chopped parsley
2 large tomatoes, skinned, deseeded and chopped
2 tbsp pine nuts, toasted until light brown in a dry pan
chopped chervil **or** parsley

MELON BASKETS
with Summer Fruits and Seafood

Ingredients
(serves 4)
2 good sized melons, Ogen, Galia or Cantaloupe for preference
2-3 oz seedless grapes, halved
1 ripe peach or nectarine, stoned and sliced thinly
4 oz cooked prawns
2 fl oz of port **or** sweet vermouth
4 tbsp greek natural yoghurt **or** crème frâiche
4 cherries
2 orange slices, halved
4 mint sprigs

Method
Place the grapes, peach slices and prawns (see note) in a bowl. Pour over the port or the vermouth and if time allows chill for 1 hour.

Stand each melon on its side and with a sharp knife starting at the centre make zig-zag cuts through to the middle of the melon all the way round. Gently pull the two halves apart and remove the seeds with their membrane. If necessary, cut a sliver from the bottom of each half to stand level.

Pack the centre of each melon with marinated fruit and prawns. Top with a tablespoon of yoghurt and garnish with a cherry, orange slice and a sprig of mint.

• If the prawns are large then cut them in half before marinating.

FRESH MANGO SALSA

Ingredients
1 large mango, peeled and chopped into small pieces
1 bunch spring onion, sliced including some green part
1 tbsp chopped fresh coriander leaves
1 dsp chilli sauce

Method
Place the mango pieces into a bowl with the finely sliced spring onions, chopped coriander and chilli sauce and mix together until thoroughly combined. Allow to chill in the fridge.

REAL RISOTTO

Method

Have the hot stock simmering gently on the hob. In a heavy saucepan gently soften the shallots in the oil and 1 oz (25g) of the butter. Add the rice and stir well to coat every grain.

Adjust the heat to moderately hot and add ¼ pint (150ml) of the hot stock and stir with a wooden spoon. As you stir and cook, the rice will absorb the stock. When it has, add the next ¼ pint (150ml) and continue the process for about 20-25 minutes or until the rice is tender but still a little firm in the centre. If you run out of stock during the cooking, hot water will suffice.

Stir in the remaining butter and the cheese. Add salt if necessary and serve at once.

Ingredients

2 pints (1¼ litres) chicken stock
2 tbsp finely chopped shallots **or** onion
½ oz (40g) butter
2 tbsp oil
10 oz (300g) raw Italian Arborio rice (see note)
2 oz (50g) freshly grated Parmesan cheese
salt to taste

• The correct type of rice is essential to this dish and most suppliers will have the word Risotto on the packet.

EGG SAUCE

Method

Melt the butter in a small pan. As soon as it foams remove from the heat, skim and add the egg, dill or parsley, lemon juice and salt to taste. Mix well. Serve at once, with steamed or baked fish.

Ingredients

4 oz (110g) unsalted butter
2 hard-boiled eggs, finely chopped
1½ tbsp chopped fresh dill **or** parsley
juice of ½ lemon
salt

PASTA, PASTA, PASTA

TAGLIATELLE VERDE with MUSHROOMS and PEAS

Ingredients

2 tbsp olive oil
2 tbsp chopped onion
4 oz (110g) bacon, diced
8 oz (225g) button mush-
   rooms, sliced
8 oz (225g) peas, cooked
salt and pepper
12 oz (350g) tagliatelle verdi,
   cooked al dente
freshly grated Parmesan
   cheese

Method

Heat the oil in a pan and add the onion and bacon and fry together for a few minutes until the bacon is just crisp and the onion is lightly browned.

Add the mushrooms and stir through to coat well and then cook for a few minutes until they are just beginning to soften. Then add the peas, mixing through well, followed by salt and pepper to taste.

Add the vegetable mixture in the pan to the hot, drained tagliatelle and toss together well. Serve at once with Parmesan cheese.

CHICKEN SALAD with BLUE CHEESE

Ingredients

8 oz (225g) cooked chicken,
   cut into cubes
4 oz (110g) seedless grapes,
   quartered
3 oz (75g) blue cheese,
   crumbled and thinly sliced
1 iceberg lettuce, shredded
6 spring onions, trimmed and
   finely sliced
8 oz (225g) pasta shells,
   cooked al dente
5 tbsp vinaigrette (made with
   lemon juice, if wished, in the
   Italian style)

Method

In a large bowl mix together the cubed chicken, grapes, blue cheese and lettuce. When well mixed together, sprinkle the spring onions over the top.

Dress the warm, drained pasta shapes with the vinaigrette and toss thoroughly. Mix the dressed pasta into the chicken salad in the bowl.

Sprinkle with the flaked almonds and serve at room temperature.

PASTA with a SPICY FRESH SALMON SAUCE

Method

Put the salmon into a large pan with the fennel, shallots, bay leaf, lemon rind and white wine. Add water to cover. Poach gently and then allow to cool in the liquid. When cooled remove the fish and break into flakes. Strain the stock and reserve.

Melt the butter in a pan and stir in the flour and curry powder until smooth. Gradually add enough of the strained stock (about ½ pint/300ml) whisking continuously, to make a thin, smooth sauce. Add salt to taste, stir through the cream and then simmer gently for 5 minutes.

Add the salmon to the sauce and serve over hot, drained pasta.

Ingredients

1 lh (450g) salmon fillet
4 fresh fennel sprigs
2 shallots, sliced
1 bay leaf
strip of lemon rind
1 small glass white wine
1 oz (25g) butter
1 level tbsp plain flour
2 level tsp mild curry powder
5 fl oz (150ml) double cream
salt
12 oz (350g) pasta, cooked al dente

ITALIAN PASTA SALAD

Method

Cook the pasta bows in plenty of boiling salted water until just tender. Drain, turn into a bowl and stir in the oil, mixed with the crushed garlic.

Add the peppers, olives and salami and mix well together. Then add the mayonnaise and mix through the salad.

Transfer to a serving bowl and garnish with green leaves and chopped parsley.

Ingredients

10 oz (275g) pasta bows
1 tbsp olive oil
1 red, green and yellow pepper, deseeded and chopped
3 oz (75g) black olives
3 pepperami salami, sliced
1 clove garlic, crushed
¼ pint (150ml) mayonnaise
green leaves and chopped parsley

STUNNING STUFFED PEPPERS

Ingredients

3 oz (75g) wild rice, cooked
with 3 oz (75g) long-grain
rice, cooked **or** 6 oz (175g)
long-grain rice, cooked
2 tbsp oil
8 spring onions, chopped,
including some green part
1 clove garlic, crushed
2 chicken breast fillets, skinned
and chopped
3 tomatoes, peeled, deseeded
and finely chopped
½ pint (300ml) chicken stock
salt and pepper
1 tbsp finely chopped parsley
2 large red peppers, halved
and deseeded
oil

Method

Heat the 2 tablespoons of oil in a pan and fry the spring onions and garlic together until softened. Remove from the pan with a slotted spoon and keep to one side.

Add the chicken to the pan and fry to seal on all sides. Return the spring onions to the pan and add the rice, stirring through well. Add the tomatoes and pour over the stock. Season to taste and then bring to the boil, cover and simmer gently until the chicken is cooked. Sprinkle with chopped parsley.

Meanwhile, brush the red peppers with oil on both sides, place them in a roasting tin and season. Bake in the oven at 400°F/200°C/gas mark 6 for 10 minutes. Then fill the peppers with the rice mixture, placing any surplus rice in an ovenproof bowl. Cover everything with foil and then bake in the oven for 15 minutes.

If wished, after 10 minutes baking, remove the foil and sprinkle grated cheese and/or toasted pine kernels or flaked almonds over the peppers and return uncovered to the oven for the remaining five minutes.

Serve with salad.

CHINA DELIGHT

PORK WITH PRAWNS

Method

Heat a large pan or flameproof casserole, add the cooking oil, then the pork and over a moderate heat stir-fry until lightly browned.

Sprinkle over the sesame oil and add the water chestnuts and pineapple chunks with their juice, followed by the soy sauce. Mix through well and then add the tomato ketchup and sugar. Mix well again adding the spring onions as you do so. Allow to boil and then simmer gently for a few minutes.

Add the prawns and stir through. Blend the cornflour with the sherry and stir into the pan. Allow to simmer and thicken for 3-4 minutes.

Serve with rice, garnished with chopped coriander leaves (or parsley).

Ingredients

1-1¼ lb (450-600g) minced pork
1 tbsp cooking oil
½-1 tsp sesame oil
8 oz (225g) can water chestnuts, drained and sliced
8 oz (225g) pineapple chunks in natural juice
2 tbsp soy sauce
4 tbsp tomato ketchup
1 dsp brown sugar
1 bunch spring onions, chopped
4 oz (110g) cooked prawns, defrosted and peeled first
4 tbsp dry sherry
2 tsp cornflour

EGG FRIED RICE

Method

In a bowl lightly beat the eggs together with 2 teaspoons of oil and 2 teaspoons of the soy sauce.

Heat a wok or deep-sided pan over a high heat, then add the oil with the white part of the spring onion. Stir-fry for a few seconds and then pour in the beaten egg mixture.

Leave for 5 seconds and then tip in the rice, turn and toss continuously (scraping the egg from the bottom) for 3-4 minutes until hot through.

Season with salt and the remaining soy sauce to taste. Add the green part of the spring onions and serve at once.

Ingredients

1 lb (450g) cold cooked rice (not chilled, made with 8 oz/ 225g raw rice)
2 eggs, lightly beaten
4 tsp soy sauce
2 tbsp oil
2 spring onions, finely cut into rounds (including equal amounts of white and green parts)
¼ tsp salt

COOL COOKING

SARDINE PATÉ

Ingredients
2 large lemons
4 oz (110g) sardines, in oil, drained
2 oz (50g) cream cheese
2 tbsp soured cream
½ tsp curry powder
1 tsp Worcestershire sauce
pepper
1 oz (25g) wholemeal bread-crumbs
2 tsp lemon juice
to garnish:
parsley
tomato wedges

Method
First cut the lemons in half, widthways in a zig-zag pattern. Scoop out the lemon flesh with a serrated knife and reserve all the juice and pulp. Cut a fine slice from the base of the lemon halves to stand them upright.

In a bowl mash together the sardines, cream cheese, soured cream, curry powder and Worcestershire sauce, adding pepper to taste. Stir in the breadcrumbs and lemon juice and then place the sardine filling into the lemon halves.

Chill until needed and then serve garnished with parsley and tomato wedges. Accompany with melba toast or crispbread.

SUMMER BERRY MOUSSE

Ingredients
1-1¼ lb (450-570g) mixed berries, (strawberries, blueberries, blackberries, raspberries)
2 tbsp red wine **or** port
3 tbsp caster sugar
12 fl oz (375ml) double cream

Method
Reserve a few of your chosen berries for garnish and place the rest of the fruit in the food processor or blender. Add the wine and sugar and blend for about 30 seconds or until the berries are just chopped.

In a large bowl beat the cream until it forms soft peaks and then fold in the berry mixture, combining it well with the whipped cream.

Place a few of the reserved berries in the base of four individual serving glasses and spoon the mousse over the top. Garnish with a sprig of fresh mint.

TUNA BEAN SALAD

Method

Rinse the beans and drain in a sieve. Place all the beans into a large bowl with the onion. Stir through carefully and then add the tuna, breaking it up into pieces with a fork.

In another bowl mix together the dressing ingredients, and when well blended together pour over the salad. Add the chopped parsley and toss together.

Spoon onto a serving dish and garnish with olives and parsley.

Ingredients

10 oz (275g) can broad beans
15 oz (425g) can cannellini
  beans
½ red skinned onion, peeled
  and finely sliced
2 x 7 oz (200g) cans tuna in oil
2 tbsp chopped parsley
for the dressing:
4 tbsp olive oil
1 tbsp red wine vinegar
Tabasco sauce **or** chilli
seasoning to taste (optional)
pepper
to garnish:
black olives
flat leaf parsley

FRESH STRAWBERRY JAM

Method

In a bowl lightly mash the strawberries with a fork, then mix in the grated zest or juice of half an orange and the caster sugar.

Very good with scones and whipped cream.

Ingredients

(serves 4)
8 oz (250g) ripe strawberries
finely grated zest or juice of
  ½ orange
2 tbsp caster sugar

CHRISTMAS QUICHE

Ingredients
(serves 6-8)

1 lb (450g) shortcrust pastry

1 lb (450g) cooked turkey **or** chicken cut into bite-sized pieces

1½ lb (700g) leeks, trimmed and finely sliced

6-7 oz (175-200g) Stilton cheese, grated or chopped

2-3 oz (50-75g) butter

salt and pepper

pinch of nutmeg

3 eggs

½ pint (300ml) double cream

Method

Roll out the pastry and use it to line a greased 10" (25.5cm) quiche or flan dish and then chill in the fridge for at least 30 minutes.

Then gently fry the leeks in the melted butter until soft. Transfer to a large bowl and add the turkey meat and Stilton and mix together with salt, pepper and nutmeg.

In a bowl beat together the eggs and cream with a fork and add to the turkey mixture, folding everything together carefully.

Fill the pastry shell with the mixture and bake in the oven at 400°F/200°C/gas mark 6 for 30-40 minutes.

Best served warm with salad.

CHRISTMAS CLASSICS

CRANBERRY RELISH

Ingredients

1 lb (450g) cranberries, fresh **or** frozen and thawed

grated rind and juice of 1 large orange

3 oz (75g) sugar

pinch of ground cinnamon

pinch of ground allspice

2 tbsp port (optional)

Method

Put the cranberries into a saucepan with the orange juice, sugar and ½ pint (300ml) water. Bring to the boil and then simmer until the fruit is cooked (about 15 minutes).

Add the spices and allow to simmer for a further 2 minutes. Remove from the heat and add the orange rind and port (if using). Cool and chill until required.

CRANBERRY SALAD

Method

In a large jug mix together the vinegar, oil, cranberry sauce, caraway seeds, celery salt and pepper, until thoroughly blended.

Place all the remaining ingredients in a large serving dish, stirring through to mix well and then pour the dressing all over the salad. Toss together lightly.

Ingredients

1 tbsp white wine vinegar
3 tbsp oil
2 tbsp cranberry sauce
½ tsp caraway seeds
½ tsp celery salt
½ tsp pepper
8 oz (225g) red cabbage, finely shredded
3 mandarin oranges, peeled and segmented
1 tbsp raisins
4 oz (110g) cucumber, cut into cubes
1 oz (25g) walnuts, roughly chopped
1 red skinned apple, cored and diced

BREAD SAUCE

Method

Use either a double saucepan or heatproof bowl over a saucepan of boiling water and into this place the butter, milk, onion, garlic, bay leaf, sage, nutmeg and seasoning.

Heat mixture until hot (but not boiling). Then add breadcrumbs and allow to continue cooking until thick and smooth. Remove the bay leaf and put through the blender or food processor.

Add cream, adjust seasoning and reheat. If the sauce is too thick, a little extra milk can be added. If the sauce has to wait, cover with a circle of parchment or foil to prevent a skin forming.

Ingredients

(serves 6)
2 oz (50g) butter
½ pint (300ml) milk
1 medium onion, roughly chopped
½ clove garlic
1 bay leaf
1 tsp dried sage
a little grated nutmeg
3 oz (75g) fresh white breadcrumbs
¼ pint (150ml) single cream
salt and pepper

SUMMER FRUITS MUESLI

Ingredients

9 oz (250g) porridge oats
1 pint (600ml) milk, (full cream is best)
2-3 tbsp honey **or** golden syrup **or** maple syrup
pinch of salt
2 oz (50g) sultanas
2 oz (50g) coarsley chopped hazelnuts
3 oz (75g) strawberries, sliced
3 oz (75g) blueberries
3 oz (75g) peeled and cut up peaches **or** nectarines
3 oz (75g) orange segments
3 oz (75g) grapefruit segments (preferably pink)
1 banana, peeled and sliced
1 tsp grated orange zest
3 oz (75g) raspberries
½ pint (300ml) cream, whipped (optional but very, very nice)

Method

Put the porridge oats into a large bowl. Add the milk, honey, salt and sultanas. Stir together well and leave to soak, covered, overnight in the refrigerator.

The next morning add the chopped nuts and all the remaining ingredients, except for the raspberries and cream, stirring through carefully.

Top with the raspberries and serve a generous dollop of cream on the side. Garnish with a sprig of mint and a dusting of icing sugar.

• A delicious combination for breakfast, brunch, lunch or even as a pudding. It's also an excellent way of coping with over-ripe or bruised fruit, since any blemishes can simply be cut out.

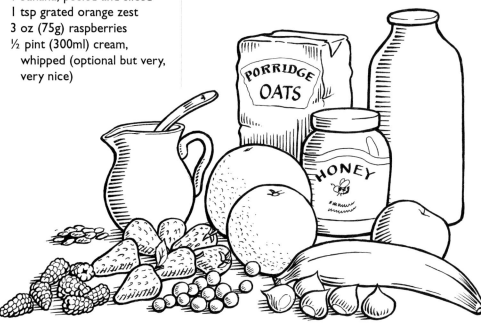

INDEX